CHAMONIX TO ZERMATT
THE WALKER'S HAUTE ROUTE

Descent to Arolla: Mont Collon
with the sharply peaked L'Évêque on its right

CHAMONIX TO ZERMATT
THE WALKER'S HAUTE ROUTE

by
Kev Reynolds

CICERONE PRESS
MILNTHORPE CUMBRIA

ACKNOWLEDGEMENTS

My thanks to Heidi Reisz of the Swiss National Tourist Office for generous assistance during the research for this book; to Daniel Bruchez, guardian of Cabane du Mont Fort, for welcome advice; and to Hedy Pollinger at Jungen who wins the gold star for hospitality. James Roberts provided additional information, and I am grateful to him. A special note of gratitude is due to Alan Payne who once again shared a long mountain trail with me, accepted my route decisions without question and patiently acted as a foreground figure to my photographs. I am thankful as ever for the continued backing of my publishers who gave me yet another excuse to spend long weeks of delight in the Alps. And to my wife and family who, with remarkable forbearance, put up with my all too-frequent absences from home, yet without whose love and support this guidebook could never have been started; sincere thanks to them all.

Kev Reynolds

Cicerone Guides by the same author:

Walks & Climbs in the Pyrenees
The Wealdway & The Vanguard Way
Walking in Kent Vols I & II
The South Downs Way & The Downs Link
The Cotswold Way
Walks in the Engadine - Switzerland
Central Switzerland
Annapurna - a Trekker's Guide
Everest - a Trekker's Guide

The Valais
The Jura (with R B Evans)
Alpine Pass Route
The Bernese Alps
Ticino

Front cover:
The Dom seen from the Toära ridge
during the descent from the Augstbord Pass

CONTENTS

Tailpiece sketches by R.B.Evans

La Sage:
Stages 8/9

INTRODUCTION

CHAMONIX TO ZERMATT, Mont Blanc to the Matterhorn. What pictures these names conjure in the minds of those of us who love mountains! The two greatest mountaineering centres in the world; one overshadowed by the highest massif in Western Europe and the other by the most famous, if not the most elegant and most instantly recognised, of all mountains.

Chamonix to Zermatt, Mont Blanc to the Matterhorn - recipe for a visual feast!

To walk from one to the other is to sample that feast in full measure; a gourmet extravaganza of scenic wonders from first day till last and each one (to carry the metaphor to its limit) a course that both satisfies and teases the palate for more.

The Walker's Haute Route does just that.

In two weeks of mountain travel you will be witness to the greatest collection of four thousand metre peaks in all the Alps and visit some of the most spectacular valleys. There you'll find delightful villages and remote alp hamlets, wander flower meadows and deep fragrant forests, skirt exquisite tarns that toss mountains on their heads, cross icy streams and clamber beside glaciers that hang suspended from huge buttresses of rock. You'll traverse lonely passes and descend into wild, stone-filled corries. There will be marmots among the boulders and ibex on the heights. And your days will be filled with wonder.

The route is 177 kilometres long. It crosses eleven passes, gains more than eleven thousand metres in height and loses more than ten thousand. And each pass gained is a window onto a world of stunning beauty.

There's the Mont Blanc range and the chain of the Pennine Alps; one massif after another of snowbound glory. Mont Blanc itself, with its organ-pipe aiguilles. The overpowering mass of the Grand Combin. Mont Blanc de Cheilon and Pigne d'Arolla, Mont Collon and Tête Blanche and the huge tooth of Dent Blanche. There's the

Grand Cornier, Ober Gabelhorn and Weisshorn and stiletto point of Zinalrothorn; there's Dom and Täschhorn, Breithorn and Matterhorn and all their crowding neighbours sheathed in ice and snow to act as the backcloth to dreams. A background landscape to the Walker's Haute Route, contender for the title of Most Beautiful Walk in Europe.

THE WALKER'S HAUTE ROUTE

THE ORIGINAL High Level Route (*Haute Route*), from Chamonix to Zermatt and beyond, was developed more than a hundred years ago. But this was very much a mountaineer's expedition, for it traced a meandering line among the great peaks of the Pennine Alps by the linking of a number of glacier passes. James David Forbes, scientist and active mountaineer, pioneered an important section of this in 1842 when he crossed the Col d'Hérens, Col de Fenêtre and Col du Mont Collon. Alfred Wills also made early explorations, but it was mainly a joint effort by other members of the Alpine Club, notably J F Hardy, William Mathews, Francis Fox Tuckett, F W Jacomb and Stephen Winkworth and their guides, that saw a complete High Level Route established in 1861. This route went from Chamonix to Col d'Argentière, then via Val Ferret, Orsières, Bourg St Pierre, Col de Sonadon, Col d'Oren, Praraye, Col de Valpelline and on to Zermatt.

The following year (1862) Col des Planards was discovered, and this led to Orsières being bypassed, thereby allowing a better line to be made in the link between the northern edge of the Mont Blanc range and that of the Pennine Alps.

This High Level Route was, of course, primarily a summer mountaineering expedition that was no small undertaking, especially when one considers the fact that at the time there were no mountain huts as we know them now and all supplies had to be carried a very long way. But with the introduction of skis to the Alps in the late nineteenth century, a new concept in winter travel

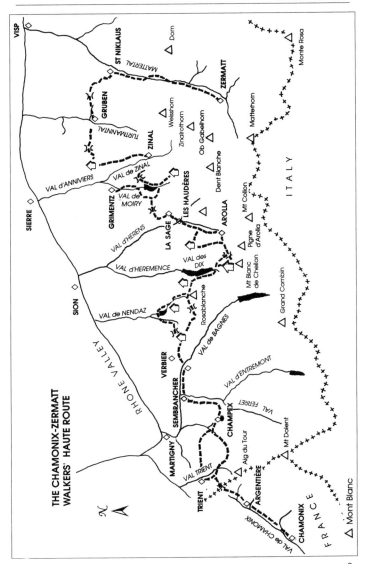

THE CHAMONIX-ZERMATT WALKERS' HAUTE ROUTE

became apparent, and the first important ski tour made in the Bernese Alps in 1897, and the subsequent winter ascent of major mountains aided by ski (Monte Rosa in 1898, Breithorn 1899, Strahlhorn 1901 etc), it was clearly only a matter of time before the challenge of the High Level Route would be subjected to winter assault.

In 1903 the first attempt was made to create a ski traverse of the Pennine Alps, and although this and other attempts failed, in January 1911 Roget, Kurz, Murisier, the brothers Crettex and Louis Theytaz succeeded in establishing a winter route from Bourg St Pierre to Zermatt.

Having successfully hijacked the original High Level Route as the ski-touring route *par excellence*, and having translated its British title as the *Haute Route*, the journey from Chamonix to Zermatt came to be seen almost universally as a winter (or more properly, a spring) expedition. A true classic that is, understandably, the focus of ambition for many experienced skiers and ski-mountaineers today.

But there's another Chamonix to Zermatt high level route that is very much a classic of its kind; a walker's route that never quite reaches three thousand metres on any of its passes, that requires no technical mountaineering skills to achieve, avoids all but a couple of minor glacier crossings (and there are alternatives to avoid even these) and yet rewards with some of the most dramatic high mountain views imaginable.

This is the Chamonix to Zermatt Walker's Haute Route.

It leads comfortably from the base of Mont Blanc to the Swiss frontier at Col de Balme, and from there down to Trient following the route of the Tour of Mont Blanc. The next pass is Fenêtre d'Arpette, leading to Champex, and from there down to the junction of Val d'Entremont and Val de Bagnes, and curving round the foot of the mountains to Le Châble. Avoiding Verbier a steep climb brings you to Cabane du Mont Fort, and continues high above the valley heading south-east before crossing three cols in quick succession in order to pass round the northern flanks of Rosablanche.

From Cabane de Prafleuri the route heads over Col des Roux and along the shores of Lac des Dix, then on to Arolla by way of Col de Riedmatten. Arolla leads to Les Haudères and up to La Sage on the green hillside above Val d'Hérens in readiness for tackling Col de Torrent. This col gives access to Val de Moiry and its hut perched in full view of a tremendous icefall, and from where the crossing of Col de Sorebois takes the walker into Val de Zinal, the upper reaches of the glorious Val d'Anniviers. From Zinal to Gruben in the Turtmanntal the route goes by way of Hotel Weisshorn, and from Gruben a final climb to the ancient crossing point of the Augstbordpass which leads directly into the Mattertal, leaving only a long but easy valley walk to Zermatt.

Every stage has its own special attributes, its own unique splendour, and all add up to a walk of classic proportions. It is, of course, a scenic extravaganza whose main features are the mountains that form the landscapes through which you walk.

First of these, of course, is dominated by the Mont Blanc massif with its towering aiguilles creating stark outlines against a backwash of snow and ice. Unbelievably high and seemingly remote from valley-based existence, the dome of the Monarch of the Alps glows of an evening, shines under a midday sun and imposes itself on panoramas viewed from cols several days' walk from the crowded boulevardes of Chamonix.

Then there's the Grand Combin making a fair imitation of its loftier neighbour as it swells above the deep cut of Val de Bagnes. This too is a vast mountain whose presence is felt many days' walk away, a grand block of glacial artistry that lures and entices from afar.

Heading round Rosablanche gives a taste of the other side of the mountain world, where gaunt screes and dying glaciers contrast the shimmering snows of its upper slopes. But then Mont Blanc de Cheilon returns the eye to grandeur on an epic scale, with Pigne d'Arolla and Mont Collon adding their handsome profiles for close inspection, while far off a first brief glimpse of the Matterhorn promises much for the future.

Val de Moiry holds many surprises with its tarn, dammed lake, majestic icefall and contorted glaciers, while Col de Sorebois and all the way down to Zinal is one long adoration of the Weisshorn. The head of Val de Zinal is so magnificent that one yearns to be able to explore further, but the route northward denies that opportunity yet allows it to be seen in true perspective; a blistering cirque that gives birth to glaciers that have carved a valley of much loveliness.

The Turtmanntal takes you back a hundred years. Above it once more rises the Weisshorn, and yet again this beautiful peak is seen in splendour from the finest viewpoint of the whole walk, which comes an hour and a half below the Augstbordpass, high above the Mattertal. The Mattertal is a long green shaft far below. Across the valley shines the Dom. Above to the right is the Weisshorn, while at the head of the valley is seen that great snowy mass which runs between Monte Rosa and the Matterhorn. But the Matterhorn keeps you waiting until the very end.

*　*　*

Despite its high passes, despite the fact that it runs across the grain of the country where deep valleys slice between the long outstretched arms of some of the highest mountains in Western Europe, the Chamonix to Zermatt route is not the sole preserve of the hardened mountain walker - although there are some taxing stages and a few delicate exposed sections that might give a twinge of concern to first-time wanderers among the Alps. Most days lead into a touch of 'civilisation', albeit sometimes this civilisation might be just a small mountain village with few amenities. Every night bar one (at Cabane de Prafleuri) there will be a lodging place with the possibility of meals provided, thereby making it unnecessary to carry camping or cooking equipment. Backpacking on this route is a choice, not an obligation. Even Cabane de Prafleuri has all the equipment needed to prepare and cook a meal, other than food itself which must be carried for a couple of days.

Lodgings on the Walker's Haute Route are in themselves very much a part of the mountain ambience. In villages they allow you to capture some of the region's culture. In remote mountain huts the wanderer is introduced to the climber's world, with an opportunity to witness high alpine scenes that are normally privy only to the mountaineer.

These lodgings vary from hotels (there are luxuriously-appointed hotels in certain villages on the route for those inclined and financially able to make use of them), to basic refuges and mattresses spread on the floor of communal dormitories in the attic of a pension or inn. There are one or two youth hostels also, for holders of a current membership card. But determined campers must understand that official campsites are not to be found in all valleys and that wild camping is officially discouraged in Switzerland.

Wherever lodgings (and campsites) are to be found along the route mention is made in the text. Similarly, wherever alternative methods of transport occur (train, bus, cable-car etc), brief details are given. This is to aid those walkers who might fall behind their schedule due to bad weather, unseasonal conditions, sickness or just plain weariness.

✳   ✳   ✳

The walk as outlined in this guide may easily be achieved within a two-week holiday. The longest stage demands only 7-7½ hours of walking (an Alternative stage elsewhere will take 8 hours, but this can be broken into two sections), while there are several days of only four hours each. Some of the less demanding days can be amalgamated by fit walkers in order to reduce the time required to complete the route, should they not have a full fortnight at their disposal. But it would be a great pity to do so. This is a walk, above all others, that ought to be wandered at a gentle pace. The very best of holidays.

This book describes the route in 14 stages with an optional extension to Saas Fee. However, the first stage (Chamonix to Argentière - 2½ hours) may be seen as a prelude. Should you arrive late in the day in Chamonix, as you would, for example, if you flew from the U.K. to Geneva and travelled from there by train, then you will probably only have sufficient time to reach Argentière on foot that day. However, if your travel arrangements get you to Chamonix at a reasonable time in the morning (by couchette on the overnight train from Paris, for example), it might be feasible to walk all the way from Chamonix to Trient, thus combining two stages for a $7^{1}/_{2}$ - 8 hour day. This effectively reduces the walk to thirteen days.

One or two commercial trekking companies from the U.K. follow a large portion of the Walker's Haute Route, but opt for public transport over some sections in order to allow a day or two in Zermatt at the end of a two week holiday. This is an option available for the individual trekker too, of course. But again, it would be a shame to miss any single stage of this route, for each bears witness to the last and forms a unique link with the next.

GETTING THERE AND BACK AGAIN

TRAVEL TO SWITZERLAND is relatively easy. Regular flights by Swissair from the U.K. are operated in conjunction with British Airways. Scheduled routes are from London (Heathrow and Gatwick) to Geneva, Basle and Zürich. Services also operate from Manchester, Birmingham and Dublin. Flight information may be obtained from Swissair, Swiss Centre, New Coventry Street, London W1V 4BJ; from British Airways, 75 Regent Street, London W1R 7HG; or from your local travel agent.

Air services from North America fly to Geneva and/or Zürich from Boston, Chicago, Los Angeles, Montreal and New York. Those airlines that maintain a routing across the Atlantic are Swissair, Trans World Airlines and Air Canada. Swissair has offices in Atlanta, Boston, Chicago, Dallas, Hartford, Houston, Los Angeles, Miami, Minneapolis, Clifton (NJ), New York, Philadelphia, San Francisco and Washington DC, and in Canada at Montreal and Toronto.

Geneva is the most convenient airport for reaching Chamonix, with which it is connected by two rail routes; one through France, the other via Martigny in the Rhône valley (change twice, once at

Martigny and again at the French border). There is also a coach service linking Geneva airport and Chamonix.

Travel by rail from the U.K. by way of the Channel ports is straightforward. French trains (SNCF) are efficient and fast. Some long-distance services do not require a change of train once boarded at a Channel port. Otherwise an overnight service from Paris to Chamonix is worth considering, for it will deliver you to the start of the route in time to enjoy a full day's walking. By booking a couchette or sleeper on this train you will arrive rested and reasonably fresh. There is a superfast TGV service from Paris to Geneva which is also worth considering. Reservations are compulsory on this and there is a fare supplement to be paid, but the speed of the service might be thought worthy of the additional fare.

Return from Zermatt at the end of the walk will be by train via Visp or Brig to Geneva (for flight) or Lausanne (connections for Paris-bound trains).

ACCOMMODATION

PRACTICALLY EVERY village along the route of this walk has a wide selection of accommodation and facilities to choose from, while between villages there are often mountain inns of one sort or another where an overnight lodging may be found. In addition there are mountain huts belonging to the Swiss Alpine Club where non-members can spend a night too. Outline details are given throughout the text wherever lodgings exist. Telephone numbers are also provided where possible to enable walkers to call ahead to reserve beds - especially important during the high season. (Note that if you are calling locally, the initial three digits of the number given in brackets ie: (087) should be ignored.)

It might also be worth noting, that the cost of accommodation in Switzerland need not be as prohibitively high as some might fear. Whilst it is pointless quoting specific prices in a guidebook that could be in print for several years, comparisons with U.K. costs are very favourable. Bed and breakfast prices in modest hotels used on this route will be on a par with charges made in British establishments, or even cheaper in some places. And a good and filling evening meal in a Swiss restaurant need cost no more than a pub meal in the U.K.

Hotel standards are high, and service will be friendly.

Dortoirs (matratzenlager in German) are highly recommended for the impecunious wanderer who does not object to a lack of privacy. Some hotels offer *dortoir* accommodation in an attic or an outbuilding; some establishments are specifically set-up as privately-run hostels. At least one of the remote mountain inns on this route has given over part of its accommodation space to a small dormitory with its own superb kitchen and bathroom facilities. In my experience these places offer value for money. They vary in style, but all provide mixed dormitory accommodation and simple washing facilities. Most have hot showers. Some have good bunk beds, others merely offer mattresses on the floor of a large room under the roof. One or two also provide the means for self-catering, whilst the majority offer a meals service. Those of us who have experience of staying in youth hostels will be more than content with the *dortoirs* on the Chamonix to Zermatt route.

There are a few youth hostels on the route. These are mentioned in the heading of each stage where they occur, but check with the International Youth Hostels Handbook (or the Swiss Youth Hostel Guide) for up-to-date information. If you plan to use hostels whilst in Switzerland, it is worth taking out membership of your home YHA in advance of your travels, as it is more expensive to join an overseas organisation. Membership of your own domestic Youth Hostels Association is recognised internationally.

Mountain huts of the SAC (Swiss Alpine Club) are also used on this route - as well as one that is privately owned. Membership of an affiliated alpine club with reciprocal rights will give reduced overnight fees. (If you are a member of the U.K. section of the Austrian Alpine Club, for example, do not forget to take your membership card with you.)

Mountain huts all offer mixed dormitory accommodation. Those used on this route provide meals and drinks. Invariably these meals are filling and high in calorific value. Washing facilities are basic and may well be non-existent in the early morning when the water supply will probably still be frozen!

On arrival at a mountain hut remove your boots before entering and help yourself to a pair of hut shoes found on a rack just inside the door. Locate the guardian to book bedspace for the night and put your name down for any meals you may require. (There will rarely be a choice of menu.) Blankets are provided in the dormitories, but a sheet sleeping bag (sleeping bag liner) is well worth carrying with you for purposes of hygiene. Remember that these huts are primarily for the use of climbers, and for many alpine routes it is necessary for mountaineers to make a very early (pre-dawn) start. Whilst your sleep may well be disturbed by those leaving early, it is important that you do not disturb others if you go to bed at night after they have settled.

As for camping, offically approved campsites are to be found in a number of valleys along the route, but certainly not in all of them. Where they do exist, facilities range from adequate to good. Off-site camping is officially discouraged in Switzerland since grasslands form a valuable part of the agricultural economy, and although it would not be beyond the bounds of possibility for individual backpackers to find a discreet corner of an alp for a single night's stay, it would be irresponsible for the guidebook writer to indicate likely sites. Wherever possible, please ask permission of farmers. It has always been my experience in Switzerland that whenever a farmer has been approached, permission has readily been granted and a good site pointed out.

In all cases, wherever you camp be discreet, take care not to foul water supplies, light no fires and pack all litter away with you.

Mention of any establishment in this book, whether as an overnight lodging or as a place where refreshments may be had, should not necessarily be taken as an endorsement of its services.

WEATHER

DESPITE THE advanced elevation of its mountains, the Valais region which our route traverses enjoys some of the best weather conditions of all Switzerland. South of the Rhône valley the average annual precipitation is considerably less than that of the Bernese Oberland, for example, in whose rain-shadow it lies. Summer temperatures are also higher than the altitude might otherwise suggest, with 25°C being not uncommon on windless days in the mountains. However, night-time temperatures can quickly plunge.

When the Föhn winds blow there will be clear skies for days at a time. But in the wake of this warm dry wind, rain should be expected. Snow can fall at any time of the year in the higher valleys and on hillsides, and in early summer particularly, thunderstorms with plenty of lightning are not at all uncommon.

Weather patterns vary from year to year and it is therefore impossible to predict with any certainty as to the likelihood of arranging a fair-weather holiday. In any case, no-one should head for the mountains and expect unlimited sunshine! But there is some comfort in the knowledge that the Pennine Alps of canton Valais receive on average a much better summer than many alpine regions, with more sunshine, higher temperatures and less rainfall than a number of other nearby centres.

July would normally be the earliest time for walkers to consider tackling this route. Before then avalanches and poor snow conditions would effectively restrict the crossing of several passes. Even early July in some years will be too soon - much depends on the amount and timing of the previous winter's snowfall. September is probably the optimum month, with crisp cold nights and bright days with clear skies.

In Switzerland, day-to-day weather forecasts may be obtained by telephone. The number to dial is 162. Local tourist information offices and guides' bureaux often display a barometer by which you can check pressure trends. Up-to-date advice may also be obtained from the guardians at mountain huts.

NOTES FOR WALKERS

THOSE WHO tackle the Chamonix to Zermatt route will find countless rewards waiting for them. Those rewards will be received at best when you are physically fit and mentally tuned. Crossing the grain of the country means that there will be many steep uphill and downhill sections to face, and since it is important to enjoy every aspect of the first pass as much as the last, fitness should be there from the very beginning.

Taking regular exercise at home will go some way towards conditioning yourself to the physical demands of the route. Of course, the best way to prepare for a walking holiday is by walking. Uphill. Carry a rucksack with a few belongings in it to accustom your shoulders to the weight. If on the first day out from Chamonix your lungs and legs scream a complaint, then you've no doubt not done enough to get fit, and the crossing of Col de Balme which deserves full enjoyment, may be an act of purgatory.

Mental fitness is as important as the physical, and often goes hand in hand with it. If you gaze with dread at the amount of height to be gained in order to cross a pass, no doubt you will suffer in consequence. Let every day be greeted with eagerness. Find joy in the steep uphill as well as the downward sloping pathway. Draw strength from the beauty of the scenes around you; enjoy the movement of clouds, the wind and wildness, as much as the gleam of sunshine; the raw crags and screes of desolation as well as the lush flower-strewn pastures and snowscapes from afar. Each is an integral part of the mountain world; a world of magic and mystery. It's a world through which it is a great privilege to move in freedom. Don't take a moment of this experience for granted.

* * *

The choice of equipment is also important. Boots need to be comfortable, fit well and be broken-in before heading for the Alps. Modern lightweight boots will be kinder to your feet at the end of the day than the traditional, heavy variety. They should give ankle support and have thick cleated soles (Vibram or similar) that are not worn smooth. You will need as much grip as possible on some sections.

Gaiters are favoured by many British hill walkers who regularly face long wet grass or boggy moorlands. In most cases gaiters will not be necessary for this route, although short ankle cuffs (stop tous) will help keep small stones and grit out of your boots.

Good waterproofs are essential, not just as protection against rain or snow, but to double as windproofs. Cagoule and over-trousers made of Goretex, or other 'breathable' materials, are recommended. Bearing in mind that some of the passes to be crossed are almost 3000 metres high, a warm pullover and/or pile jacket should also be taken, as should a woollen hat or balaclava, and gloves.

If one needs to be prepared for the wet and cold, it is also necessary to take action against long periods of extreme sun and unshaded heat. Suncream (factor 6 or stronger) and sunglasses should be part of your equipment.

A first aid kit must be included. Water bottle, compass, headtorch and spare batteries, whistle and maps should also be taken, as should a small amount of emergency food. (This can be recharged regularly as you pass through a village.) A sheet sleeping bag (sleeping bag liner) is highly recommended for use in *dortoirs* and mountain huts. A sleeping bag will not be required though.

An ice-axe may prove extremely useful. Since no-one can predict what weather conditions will be faced, you should be prepared for snow or ice to be lying in shaded corries, particularly on the approach to, or descent from, a high pass. An ice-axe - and the knowledge of how to use it as a brake in case of a fall - may prove to be a valuable item of equipment and well worth the weight and inconvenience of carrying it.

A well-fitting rucksack with a waist-belt adjusted to take the weight of the pack is important. It need not be very large, since you should be able to keep equipment down to a minimum, unless your plan is to backpack with full camping and cooking gear. A large, thick polythene bag in which to pack all your equipment inside the sack will protect items from getting wet in the event of bad weather. A selection of plastic bags of assorted sizes will also be useful.

* * *

A word about drinking water in the mountains. Whilst I have never personally suffered any problems from drinking directly from clear mountain streams, it is probably wise to restrict topping-up your water bottles from either your overnight lodging or from one of the many hewn-out log troughs that are found on grassy alps. These troughs, mainly for cattle, are nonetheless filled directly by a spring-fed pipe, and the gushing fountain should be perfectly safe for human consumption.

* * *

On all but the last two days of the walk the route passes through French-speaking territory, but once you cross the Meidpass (Stage 12) German becomes the official language. Although the non-linguist may have difficulty conversing in general with locals met in the mountains, English is widely understood in most of the villages, and you will probably face no real language problems in hotels or other lodgings. Appendix E contains a glossary of French and German words likely to be met along the way. But it is no substitute for either a pocket dictionary or a phrase-book.

PATHS AND WAYMARKS

MOST OF THE paths on this route will have been in use for centuries by farmers, traders and hunters going about their daily business - from alp to alp, or from one valley to the next by way of an ancient pass, or up onto a ridge where chamois or ibex might be spotted. A few may be of recent origin, either laid out by a local commune, by a branch of the Swiss Footpath Protection Association *(Schweizerische Arbeitsgemeinschaft für Wanderwege)*, by the Valais Rambling Association *(Walliser Vereinigung für Wanderwege)* or by members of the SAC in order to reach a mountain hut.

There are two official types of footpath in Switzerland which are signposted and waymarked to a common standard. A *Wanderweg* (*chemin pedestre*) is a path that remains either in the valley, or along the hillsides at a modest altitude. These are maintained and graded at a more gentle angle than the *Bergweg*, or *chemin de montagne*. Yellow metal signposts contain the names of major landmark destinations, such as a pass, lake, hut or village, often with estimated times given in hours (*Heures* in French, *Stunden* in German-speaking regions) and minutes (*Min*). A white plate on these yellow signs names the immediate locality and, sometimes, the altitude. Along the trail occasional yellow signs or paint flashes on rocks are found.

A mountain path (*chemin de montagne*, or *Bergweg*) is one which ventures higher and is more demanding than the *Wanderweg*. These paths will usually be rougher, narrower, and sometimes fading if not in regular use. Signposting will be similar to that already described, except that the outer sections of the finger post will be painted red and white, and the intermediate paint flashes along the way will be blazed white-red-white. Occasional cairns may also be used to direct the way over boulder slopes, or where poor visibility could create difficulties. In the event of mist or low cloud obscuring the onward route, it is essential to study the area of visibility with the utmost care before venturing on to the next paint flash or stone-built cairn. In extreme cases it may be necessary to take compass bearings and make progress from one to the other in this manner.

Note: At no point along the walk will you find a sign that mentions the Chamonix-Zermatt Haute Route.

SAFETY IN THE MOUNTAINS

WHILST THE ROUTE is mostly well signposted and with good paths, and there are working farms and villages at frequent intervals along the way, there are some wild and remote sections where an accident could have serious consequences. Mountains contain a variety of objective dangers for the unwary and the long distance walker should be prepared to cope with any hazards that arise.

Plan each day's walk carefully. Study the route outline, the amount of height to be gained and lost, and the time required to reach your destination. None of the stages described are particularly long, but in case you are tempted to double up, make sure you have enough hours of daylight in which to cross the day's pass and descend to the safety of the next valley, or to where a night's lodging may be had, before nightfall. Carry a few emergency food rations and a first aid kit. Know how to read both a map and compass, and watch for signs of deteriorating weather. Never be too proud to turn back if it is safer to do so than to continue in the face of an on-coming storm.

In the unhappy event of an accident, stay calm. Should the party be large enough to send for help whilst someone remains with the injured member, make a careful written note of the precise location where the victim can be found. If there is a mountain hut or farm nearby, seek assistance there. If valley habitation is nearer, find a telephone and dial **01 383 11 11**. This calls out the Swiss Air Rescue - **but should only be used if absolutely essential.**

The international distress call is a series of six signals (either blasts on a whistle, or flashes of a torch after dark) spaced evenly for a minute, followed by one minute's pause, then repeated with a further six signals. The reply is three signals per minute followed by a minute's pause.

Note: There is no free mountain rescue service in Switzerland, and no free hospital treatment. Emergencies will therefore be extremely costly. Specialist mountain insurance companies frequently advertise in the outdoor press in Britain, and some standard holiday insurance policies can often be extended to include mountain walking in the Alps. But do check the small print for exclusion clauses and make sure the cost of rescue (if required) is covered. Be insured, and be cautious.

FLORA AND FAUNA

THE PENNINE ALPS contain the richest flora in all Switzerland. One of the factors responsible for this is the mixture of limestone, gneiss and schistose rocks, which encourage calcipile (lime-loving) plants to flourish in some areas, calcifuge varieties in others. Climatic considerations also play an important role, as does the difference in altitude between valley bed and the limit of the upper plant zone. Walkers who daily cross the high passes in a traverse of the region - particularly in the early summer - will wander through a number of successive plant zones, and it is not at all necessary to be a trained botanist to enjoy the flushing variety of flowers and shrubs on show. There are, however, several handy well-illustrated guidebooks available that provide at-a-glance information as to specific flowers likely to be seen. Walkers with a particular interest may find the weight of either *The Alpine Flowers of Britain and Europe* by Christopher Grey-Wilson and Marjorie Blamey (Collins 1979) or *Mountain Flowers* by Anthony Huxley (Blandford Press 1967), worth carrying in the rucksack for identification purposes.

There will be all the expected varieties, from gentian to edelweiss, from alpenrose to crimson-eyed primulas, and many more besides. This is not the place to list them all. Newcomers to the Alps may be surprised to find that it is not only the meadowlands that fire with bloom, but that even the high, seemingly lifeless cliff faces, screes and glacier-bordering moraines have their own species of flowering plant, and it is often such discoveries that make days in the mountains additionally memorable.

A number of alpine plants are highly protected. Post Offices (PTT), some hotels and tourist information offices frequently display posters indicating these varieties. There are also Plant Protection Zones in certain valleys where it is forbidden to pick any of the plants. But whether protected by law or not, the best way to collect alpine flowers is firstly through the senses, and then by way of the camera lens. Others may then share the pleasures they first brought you.

*   *   *

Of all creatures native to the Alps the one most likely to be seen on this walk is the marmot (*Marmota marmota*). On many days you will no doubt first hear a sharp shrill whistle as you cross a boulder slope or wander over a high alp on the borders of grassland and scree. This is the marmot's warning cry, and you may then see two or three brown, furry creatures scurrying for cover.

The marmot is a gregarious animal, living in colonies among a variety of mountain and valley locations in burrows whose entrance holes may be seen from some of the footpaths on the walk. They grow to the size of a large hare and weigh up to ten kilograms, hibernating in winter for around five months, then emerging in spring when the snow cover melts. Their young are born during the early summer and you may be lucky enough to catch sight of two or three kitten-sized creatures romping or playfully fighting in the short grass of the upper hillsides.

Chamois (*Rupicapra rupicapra*) are rarely seen at close quarters, but in the high regions of the mountains, just below the snowline, it is not unusual to spy a small herd picking its way with commendable ease over excessively steep terrain. From a distance it is possible to mistake chamois, with their small curving horns, for female or young ibex. Ibex, however, have a stockier body.

Ibex (*Capra ibex*) are also known as *bouquetin* (French) or *steinbock* (German). These squat, sturdy animals live and graze in herds; one noble buck with a harem of females. The male sports a pair of majestic scimitar-shaped horns marked with a series of knobbles, like arthritic joints. These horns are used in battle as they fight for control over the herds, usually in the autumn.

On the scenic belvedere path from Cabane du Mont Fort to Col Termin, known as the Sentier des Chamois (Stage 6), ibex are likely to be seen from close quarters. A large herd lives nearby on a hillside designated as a wildlife sanctuary. Another herd may be seen near Cabane de Prafleuri.

RECOMMENDED MAPS

MAPS OF THE Swiss survey, *Landeskarte der Schweiz* (L.S. or *Carte nationale de la Suisse*), are among the finest in the world. By artistic use of shading, contours and colouring, the line of ridges and rock faces, the flow of glaciers and streams, the curve of an amphitheatre, narrow cut of a glen, the expanse of a lake and forest cover of a hillside all announce themselves clearly. A picture of the country immediately leaps from the paper.

At the head of each stage of the walk a note is given with regard to the specific map recommended for that particular stretch. In each case I have chosen the 1:50,000 series, as this should be perfectly adequate for most needs. The greater detail provided by the 1:25,000 series is not likely to be required on this route, given the amount of waymarking on the ground. (No less than 9 sheets would be needed of 1:25,000 scale.)

Standard coverage at 1:50,000 scale runs into 4 sheets (numbers 282, 283, 273 and 274), but we are fortunate in that the L.S. has published a double-sheet coverage for this particular area, so only two sheets are actually needed. These are:

5003 Mont Blanc - Grand Combin
5006 Matterhorn - Mischabel.

Addresses of map suppliers are given in Appendix C.

USING THE GUIDE

A BRIEF WORD of explanation about this guidebook. Distances are given throughout in kilometres and metres. Heights quoted are in metric too. These details are taken directly from the map, but in attempting to measure the actual distance of each day's walk I have made the nearest estimation I could. (With countless zig-zags it is impossible to be precise.) Likewise, times are approximate only and make no allowances for rest stops or photographic interruptions. Inevitably these times will be found slow by some walkers, fast by others. By comparing your times with those given here (and quoted on signposts along the route) you will soon discover how much our pace differs and adjustments can then be made when calculating your own progress through the day.

Throughout the text route directions 'left' and 'right' apply to the direction of travel, whether in ascent, descent or traverse. However, when used with reference to the banks of glaciers or streams, 'left' and 'right' indicate the direction of flow, ie: looking downwards. Where doubts might occur a compass direction is also given.

I have attempted to avoid an over-use of abbreviations in the guide, but it is inevitable that some have been adopted. All should be straightforward and easily understood, but the following list is given for clarification:

kms........	kilometres
L.S....	Landeskarte der Schweiz (maps)
m......	metres
mins... ...	minutes
PTT........	Post Office (Post, Telephone & Telegraph)
SAC..... ...	Swiss Alpine Club
TGV.......	Trains à Grande Vitesse (the French superfast train)

✳   ✳   ✳

Finally, I have made every effort to check the route as described for accuracy, and it is to the best of my belief that the guidebook goes into print with all details correct. However, changes do occur from time to time with paths re-routed and certain landmarks altered. Any corrections required to keep the book up-to-date will be made in future printings where possible. Should you discover any changes that are necessary (or can recommend additions with regard to accommodation, places of refreshment etc) I would very much appreciate a brief note to that effect. A postcard sent to me via the publisher would be gratefully received.

ROUTE PROFILE KEY

 accommodation: hotel, dortoir, youth hostel, mountain hut

 Official campsite

 Refreshments: food and/or drinks

 Bus service

 Railway station

 Cable car

 Gondola lift

3 hrs 45 mins | Walking time from start of stage

All heights in metres

STAGE 1:
CHAMONIX - ARGENTIÈRE

Distance:	10 kilometres
Time:	2¹/₂ hours
Start altitude:	1037m *High point:* Argentière 1251m
Height gain:	214m
Map:	L.S. 5003 Mont Blanc - Grand Combin 1:50,000
Accommodation:	Chamonix - hotels, camping
	Les Praz de Chamonix (30 mins) - camping
	Le Lavancher (1¹/₂ hours) - hotel
	Argentière - hotels, gîte
Transport options:	Train & bus (Chamonix-Argentière)

This initial, very short stage, is suggested as a prelude for walkers who arrive in Chamonix late in the day and who wish to get a bit of countryside under their boots before looking for overnight accommodation. Those who arrive early and fresh enough from their travels can, of course, combine this with Stage 2 and continue over Col de Balme to Trient for an eight-hour day.

It's a valley walk without any passes to tackle. But it's a pleasant valley walk all the same, with one or two short ascents to contend with. It begins by threading a way among the crowds that throng the streets of Chamonix and heads upvalley on the road leading out of town, but then takes to a woodland path alongside the river. Most of the way journeys among woods on the southern side of the valley; the best part of the route being that which follows the so-called Petit Balcon Nord. For the most part views of the big mountains are shielded, but when they do appear, they are worth pausing to admire.

Chamonix's valley, the valley of the Arve, is dominated by the Mont Blanc massif whose jagged aiguilles form fenceposts of granite and whose huge glaciers hang in sheets of arctic splendour above the town and its

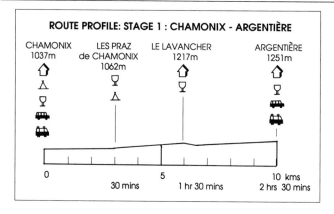

ROUTE PROFILE: STAGE 1 : CHAMONIX - ARGENTIÈRE

neighbouring forests. The northern wall, however, is much more bare, with the Aiguilles Rouges holding its upper reaches.

As early as 1741 Chamonix - then a small village - was 'discovered' by Richard Pococke and William Windham, whose Account of the Glaciers or Ice Alps in Savoy *sowed the seeds of popularity for the valley; a popularity that has steadily increased from a lowly trickle to the present-day deluge of tourists who threaten an overkill with almost a million visitors per year in Chamonix alone.*

Footpaths along the valley are busy during the summer, and will remain so for the first three stages; that is until the route of the Tour of Mont Blanc (TMB) has been left behind. During the high season accommodation is likely to be heavily used.

* * *

[1] **CHAMONIX** (1037m) *Hotels, camping, restaurants, shops, banks, PTT, tourist information, railway, buses, cableways and funicular.* From Chamonix railway station walk down the main street, [2] Avenue Michel Croz, among shops and restaurants, and take the first road breaking away to the right. This is [3] Rue Whymper, with a small garden on the corner. Continue straight ahead along the road which is signposted to Les Praz and Argentière, and you will soon leave the town behind.

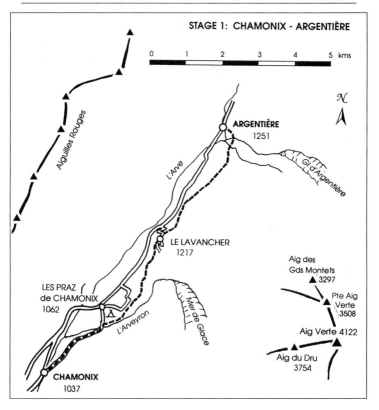

STAGE 1: CHAMONIX - ARGENTIÈRE

ARGENTIÈRE 1251

Aiguilles Rouges

L'Arve

Gd. d'Argentière

LE LAVANCHER 1217

LES PRAZ de CHAMONIX 1062

L'Arveyron

Mer de Glace

Aig des Gds Montets ▲ 3297

Pte Aig Verte 3508

Aig Verte 4122

Aig du Dru 3754

CHAMONIX 1037

After about two kilometres this road veers left and crosses the Arveyron, the river which drains the great icefield of the Mer de Glace. The village of **LES PRAZ de CHAMONIX** (1062m 30 mins *camping*) lies a short distance along the road.

Immediately across the river head to the right on a pathway signposted as the *Promenade des Bourses*, ducking beneath the railway and wandering ahead through woods beside the river. As you make progress there are several alternative paths and tracks branching away, but you continue upvalley in the same direction as before. On coming to signs for Le Lavancher and Les Tines the trail begins to climb, mostly among trees.

As you draw near to **LE LAVANCHER** (1217m 1 hour 30 mins *hotel, restaurant*) follow footpath signs indicating the Petit Balcon Nord to Argentière. This footpath goes through the small community of Le Lavancher, across open meadows (a prime viewpoint down valley to Mont Blanc) and through woods, gaining height at times, but also following a gentle contour at others. It is a most pleasant walk, with signs now mostly indicating either Petit Balcon or Argentiere.

After about 2¹/₂ hours from Chamonix you come to **ARGENTIÈRE** on the main valley road.

[4] **ARGENTIÈRE** (1251m *hotels, gîte d'étape (le Belvedere 74400 Argentière-tel/fax 50540259), restaurants, shops, PTT, tourist information, railway and bus links with Chamonix, cableways etc*)

Note: In case of difficulty finding accommodation here, try Les Moulins des Frasserands (*dortoir - breakfasts available, but no evening meals*), about 2 kms upvalley.

✳   ✳   ✳

Places or Features of Interest Along the Way:

1. **CHAMONIX**: With the close proximity of Mont Blanc, Chamonix has always been at the forefront of alpine mountaineering, and during the development of alpinism in the 19th century became a serious rival to Zermatt. Today it is unquestionably the leading mountaineering centre of Europe, if not the world. But the town's importance is spread beyond the limits of mountaineering, for in winter it is a major ski resort, while in summer Chamonix attracts a veritable deluge of general tourists. It has plenty to occupy them, including the cable-car to the summit of the Aiguille du Midi, and from there the possibility of traversing the whole range by cableway to Entrèves, near Courmayeur in Italy. The railway to Montenvers

The full majesty of the Grand Combin is seen from the Sentier des Chamois on the way to the Grand Désert (Stage 6)

has long been one of the most popular excursions, with its climax being the superb views to be had along the Mer de Glace to the Grandes Jorasses. The Chamonix valley, of course, offers superb walking. (For a guidebook to the walking potential of the area see *Chamonix-Mont Blanc* by Martin Collins [Cicerone Press]). Although the classic Tour du Mont Blanc does not actually visit Chamonix itself, it does traverse the valley. (See *The Tour of Mont Blanc* by Andrew Harper [Cicerone Press])

2. **MICHEL CROZ**: The Haute Route begins by wandering down Avenue Michel Croz in Chamonix. This is named after one of the finest guides of the Golden Age of Mountaineering, a man whose talent and skills were discovered by Alfred Wills and then put to good use by Edward Whymper. Croz was a Chamonix guide (born at Le Tour in 1830) whose first ascents included the Ecrins, Mont Dolent, Aiguille d'Argentière, Dent Blanche, Grandes Jorasses and the crossing of the Moming Pass above Zinal. In 1865 Croz was in Whymper's party to make the first ascent of the Matterhorn, but was one of those tragically killed on the descent.

3. **EDWARD WHYMPER**: On leaving Avenue Michel Croz the route turns into Rue Whymper. Whymper, of course, will forever be remembered as the man who first climbed the Matterhorn, and as such is known far beyond the somewhat limited circle of active mountaineers. Whymper was a London-born wood engraver who first visited the Alps in 1860 in order to make a series of sketches for the publisher, William Longman. The following year he began a remarkable climbing career (often with Michel Croz) that included first ascents of the Barre des Ecrins, the aiguilles of Trélatête and Argentière, Grand Cornier, Grandes Jorasses (West summit), Aiguille Verte and, of course, the Matterhorn. He did little climbing in the Alps after the Matterhorn tragedy, but explored farther afield - making journeys to Greenland, the Andes of South America and

In the Val de Nendaz; an alternative to crossing the Grand Désert (Alternative Stage 6)

three trips to the Canadian Rockies. His *Scrambles Amongst the Alps* is still considered to be one of the finest of all mountaineering books. Whymper died in Chamonix at the age of 71.

4. **ARGENTIÈRE**: A compact village at the upper end of the Chamonix valley, attractive in places, but in danger of being swamped by modern architectural developments indicative of those that grow around ski resorts. It has a range of accommodation possibilities, including a gîte d'étape for walkers with limited finances. Plenty of restaurants and food stores, and a tourist information office.

STAGE 2:
ARGENTIÈRE - COL de BALME - TRIENT

Distance:	12 kilometres	
Time:	5-5¹/₂ hours	
Start altitude:	1251m	*High point:* Col de Balme 2204m
Height gain:	953m	*Height loss:* 925m
Map:	L.S. 5003 Mont Blanc - Grand Combin 1:50,000	
Accommodation:	Le Tour (1 hour 30 mins) - hotel	
	Col de Balme (3 hours) - refuge	
	Trient - hotels, dortoir	
Transport options:	Bus (Argentière-Le Tour)	
	Cableway (Le Tour-Les Grandes Otanes,	
	near Col de Balme)	

For a first full day's walking this is a most convenient stage. There's plenty of height to gain and lose, but Col de Balme is not at all severe and walkers fresh out from the U.K. have an opportunity to get into their stride painlessly. Views on the way to the pass, when you look back through the length of the Chamonix valley, are dominated by Mont Blanc and its aiguilles, while the col itself gives a most magnificent vision of the Monarch of the Alps shining its great snow dome and sending down long glacial tentacles into the valley.

The Swiss frontier runs through Col de Balme, so all the descent (and the rest of the walk to Zermatt) will be within Swiss territory. Vistas of Mont Blanc are shunted into memory, although in days to come sudden surprise views will draw the eye back to the west where a crown of snow reveals that remembered glory once more.

The valley of Trient into which you descend is a green and pastoral stretch of tranquillity. There are no great peaks nearby, of either snow or rock, to match the grandeur of France behind you, but the scene is not short of its splendours and off to the north a line of mountains indicates the crest

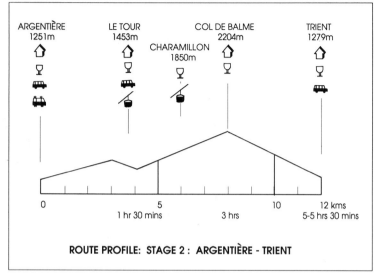

ROUTE PROFILE: STAGE 2 : ARGENTIÈRE - TRIENT

of the Bernese Alps, with Wildhorn and Wildstrubel just discernible. The descent is one to enjoy for itself.

Much of this stage is shared with the route of the Tour of Mont Blanc, so you will no doubt meet plenty of other walkers during the day.

✳   ✳   ✳

From the centre of Argentière take the road heading off to the right (east), passing the PTT and crossing the river (l'Arve) with the [1] Glacier d'Argentière seen hanging from its great shelf directly ahead. At a junction of streets bear right and you will soon come to the valley's railway line. Pass beneath this and onto a track ahead, going towards woods. Here you rejoin the Petit Balcon Nord and after a few metres bear left by a chalet. The route is signposted to Le Tour and Le Planet.

Rising steadily among trees you will come to a junction of paths (**LES AUGES** 1412m) and continue straight ahead. Soon emerging from the woods the path narrows and gradually loses height. The village of Le Tour is seen below, Col de Balme directly ahead, while

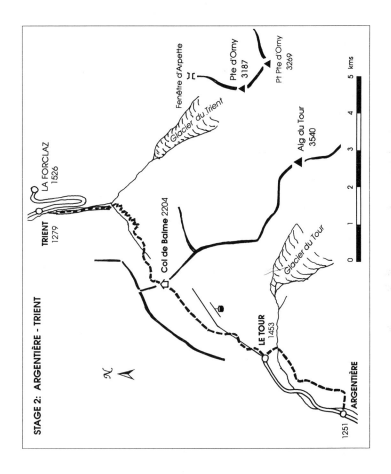

STAGE 2: ARGENTIÈRE - TRIENT

across the valley to the west the Aiguilles Rouges appear rather fine.

The path brings you down to a stream that has recently come from the Glacier du Tour, and you cross this by way of a footbridge and walk on into the little village of **LE TOUR** (1453m 1¹/₂ hours *hotel, gîte (CAF-owned) restaurant, water supply, public toilets, telephone, bus to Chamonix, gondola lift*). *Note*: If you prefer to take the easy way to Col de Balme, ride the gondola lift to its upper station at Les Grandes Otanes, from which a short and easy walk leads on an even contour to the pass.

The route to the col continues by passing along the right-hand side of the gondola lift station, and straight ahead on a broad track/ski piste. Before long a waymarked footpath breaks away to the right (it is signposted) where you enjoy fine views to Mont Blanc. This now climbs easily up to the middle station of the gondola lift (**CHARAMILLON** 1850m *refreshments*). There is a junction of paths, with the right-hand trail heading off to the popular Albert Premier Hut below the Aiguille du Tour. Ignore this option and continue straight ahead and, gaining height without undue effort, reach **COL de BALME** (2204m 3-3¹/₂ hours *accommodation, refreshments*). The unmarked Franco/Swiss border runs across the pass, with the refuge standing on the Swiss side of the frontier. (Purchases may be made in either French or Swiss francs. Prices, however, are Swiss.)

Superb views are to be had from here, especially south to the great snowy mass of [2] Mont Blanc and its guardian aiguilles. The Verte and Dru stand side by side, while the Chamonix Aiguilles stab skywards in stark gesticulations against the gleaming snows. The Aiguilles Rouges are only rouge in certain light conditions, but their rocky presence adds to the scene.

Groups of ebullient walkers occupied the seats outside the refuge, and inside too. To a man they were all tackling the TMB and enjoying the cameraderie such a walk inspires, greeting each new arrival with rude remarks, having established an easy rapport over several days during which they'd shared the same paths, valleys and passes. They were all heading south on the closing stages of their classic walk. We were going in the opposite direction, against the tide, as it were, with two weeks of activity ahead. Two weeks of wandering, with more beauty in store than any wanderer had a right to expect. Two weeks of known and unknown, of mountains and valleys familiar from previous visits, and others that were completely unfamiliar as yet. I gazed back at the glory that was Mont Blanc but regretted not its passing, for ahead lay a savage grid of ridges that teased and enticed. That first pass, the Col de Balme, was the key to a wonderland.

Veer left beyond the refuge to a signpost at a footpath junction, then go right to begin the descent proper. (Trient is 2 hours from the col.) The path goes down in long loops at first, but once you enter forest the way steepens with tighter zig-zags. It brings you into a rough pastureland where you bear left to cross the Nant Noir stream and walk down to the nearby village of **TRIENT**.

(3) **TRIENT** (1279m 5-5¹/₂ hours) *Accommodation (Hotel du Glacier, dortoir in Relais du Mont Blanc - Tel: (026) 22 46 23) and Le Café Moret (026) 222707) restaurants, food store, PTT, Postbus link with Martigny. Office du Tourisme, 1921 Trient (Tel: 026 22 19 29). Just before you enter Trient, note Refuge du Peuty (gîte) on left.*

Note: In case of difficulty in finding accommodation here, try Hotel du Col de la Forclaz 3 kms uphill to the east. Bedrooms and dortoir. (Tel: (026) 22 26 88)

❋   ❋   ❋

Places or Features of Interest Along the Way:
1. **GLACIER d'ARGENTI'ERE**: This major icefield flows from the great basin formed by the curving ridges of the Tour Noir, Mont Dolent, Aiguille de Triolet, Les Courtes and Les Droites. Mont Dolent is the lynchpin of this system, and on its summit the frontiers of France, Italy and Switzerland meet.

2. **MONT BLANC**: As the highest mountain in Western Europe Mont Blanc (4807m) has been the focus of mountaineering attention for more than two centuries. In 1760 De Saussure offered a prize to the first man who would reach its summit. Several attempts were made in the ensuing years, but it was not until 8 August 1786 that

Michel-Gabriel Páccard, the Chamonix doctor, and Jacques Balmat, a crystal hunter, reached the top. Tourist ascents followed, then attention was focussed on neighbouring aiguilles and new routes to already claimed summits. Among the outstanding developments mention should be made of the Brenva Ridge in 1865, Peuterey Ridge (1927), Route Major (1928), Gervasutti Pillar (1951) and Central Pillar of Freney in 1961. But whilst practically every face, pillar, ridge and couloir has been explored, Mont Blanc today still manages to retain its charisma, and to non-mountaineers no less, its undisputed grace and beauty. (For a history of the mountain see *Savage Snows* by Walt Unsworth [Hodder & Stoughton, 1986])

3. **TRIENT**: A small village set in a narrowing of the valley of the same name below La Forclaz. In spite of its being the first Swiss habitation met on this walk, it is nonetheless very French in both architecture and atmosphere. It is in an ideal situation to tackle the crossing of the Fenêtre d'Arpette, an alternative to which goes to Champex by way of La Forclaz and the so-called 'Bovine' route - part of the TMB. (See Alternative Stage 3)

Le Tour, dominated by the Glacier du Tour

STAGE 3:
TRIENT - FENÊTRE d' ARPETTE - CHAMPEX

Distance:	14 kilometres
Time:	6¹/₂-7 hours
Start altitude:	1279m *High point:* Fenêtre d'Arpette 2665m
Height gain:	1386m *Height loss:* 1199m
Map:	L.S. 5003 Mont Blanc - Grand Combin 1:50,000
Accommodation:	Arpette (6 hours) - hotel/dortoir, camping
	Champex - hotels, pension, dortoirs, youth hostel,
	camping
Transport options:	Postbus (Trient-Col du Forclaz-Martigny)
	Train (Martigny-Orsières)
	Bus (Orsières-Champex)

The crossing of Fenêtre d'Arpette is a classic outing and one of the most demanding of the whole walk. The approach to it is full of interest with the frozen cascades of the Glacier du Trient's icefall in view nearly all the way, while the descent from this rocky pass into the lovely pastoral Val d'Arpette begins with a wild and untamed wilderness of scree and boulders, but finishes with joyful streams, spacious woods and meadows. These contrasts are bound to bring pleasure to all Haute Route trekkers, for it is in such contrasts that long distance mountain routes gain much of their appeal.

The path is a good one practically all the way, but care should be exercised on the descent from the pass where boulder fields are crossed. A twisted ankle could have serious consequences.

At the end of the day Champex is the first 'real' Swiss village of the route, with attractive chalets facing the sun and boxes of flowers at the windows. It's a popular, welcoming little resort that has grown along the shores of a small reedy lake, and is noted for its magnificent alpine garden - considered by many to be the finest in Switzerland.

Note: *An alternative approach to Champex, less demanding than the*

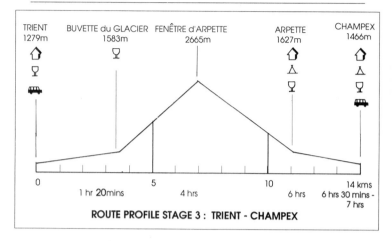

ROUTE PROFILE STAGE 3 : TRIENT - CHAMPEX

Arpette crossing, yet a very pleasant walk in its own right, is the so-called 'Bovine' route also adopted by the Tour of Mont Blanc. In particularly bad weather conditions it would be preferable to the more rigorous high crossing of the Fenêtre d'Arpette. See Alternative Stage 3 for a brief description of the route.

From the church in Trient go up to the main Col de la Forclaz road and turn right. On the edge of the village bear left by a stone cross onto a broad track rising in gentle zig-zags through forest. At a junction of tracks continue ahead to reach the road. Cross directly ahead onto the continuing grass track which soon narrows to a footpath, zig-zags again and comes to a lovely *bisse* path where you turn right. (A *bisse* is an irrigation water course.) Follow this path all the way to **BUVETTE du GLACIER** (1583m 1hr 20mins *refreshments*).

The path forks here and you bear left, climbing uphill to another fork. Once more you take the left branch (the right-hand, lower, path goes to the glacier) where the climb to the pass begins in earnest, first among woods, then above these on a more open stretch with clear uninterrupted views onto the contortions of the glacier. As you gain height so the Aiguilles Dorées and Pointe d'Orny grow

42

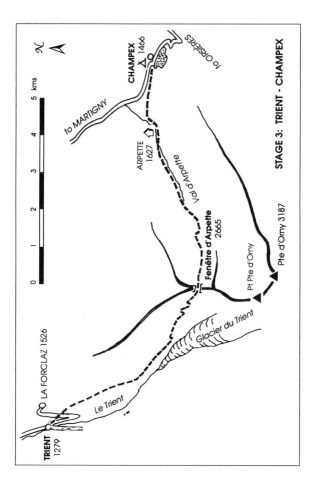

STAGE 3: TRIENT - CHAMPEX

above you to the south.

The way steepens considerably in places, but the path is always clearly defined, even when crossing rocky slopes. Few paths allow such detailed study of an icefield in all its tortured glory as this does, and views are consistently magnificent. But the pass remains a well-kept secret until you're almost there.

A last scramble over a jumble of rocks brings you finally to the **FENÊTRE d'ARPETTE** (2665m 4 hours). This wild and rocky perch makes a splendid pass, for the ridge it breaches is very much a division; to the west all mountains and glaciers owe allegiance to Mont Blanc, while to the east lies a new world - a stony world, not an arctic one, and it will be two more days before you again feel the brush of glacial air on your face. The two-day intermission goes from bare rocks to pasture and forest, through a neat and tended landscape, a brief respite before the high mountain fastnesses are once more regained. Fenetre d'Arpette is a geological hyphen, and from it you gaze eagerly to the east and south-east where a great array of ridges jostle the horizon and the Combin massif gleams a splash of white against the sky. A promise of good things to come.

We reached the pass in time to eat our lunch, emerging from a cool wind to bright sunshine and sun-warmed rocks on the Arpette side. But the walking world had come to the Fenêtre too, for everywhere we looked tanned bodies were spread across the rocks like basking seals. Not for nothing is this pass known locally as the Champs d'Elysses. Thank the popularity of the Tour of Mont Blanc for that, for this pass is on a much-loved Variante. Ten thousand people a year walk that grand circuit. How was I to know they would all be gathered that very day on the Fenêtre d'Arpette?

At first the descent drops into a rough, stony bowl at the head of Val d'Arpette. Caution is advised for the initial 100 metres or so where each one of an assortment of paths is particularly steep and, at times, loose under foot. Below this you cross a tumbled boulder field before the path (waymarked over the boulders) treats you with more respect and eases into Val d'Arpette proper.

Pastures and fruiting shrubs are a welcome relief after the barren rocks of the higher valley, and in almost two hours from the pass

The Trient Glacier seen from the Fenêtre d'Arpette

you come to a group of farms where a track leads onto the right bank of the stream. Five minutes later you reach the **RELAIS d'ARPETTE** (1627m 6 hours *accommodation [beds & dortoir], camping, refreshments Tel: (026) 83 12 21).*

Just beyond the hotel turn off the main track/road and take a footpath on the left that descends among trees and follows a stream. On coming to a bridge cross over, then go right on a footpath waymarked with green stripes. Recross the stream and soon after bear left when the path forks.

The fast-running brook you now accompany is a leat, or *bisse* - a watercourse created to direct part of a stream into a new valley, or to bring water to otherwise dry farmland. The Valais region has many such watercourses, and the Chamonix-Zermatt route will follow more of them in the days ahead. This one is a delight, a cheerful companion that sings as it scurries along its shallow bed.

The path eventually brings you out of the woods at a small pond by a chairlift station. Go onto the road and bear right into **CHAMPEX**. (If you require youth hostel accommodation, head to the left for 1 km to reach the Auberge de la Jeunesse - Chalet Bon Abris Tel: (026) 83 14 23)

[2] ***CHAMPEX*** *(1466m 7 hours) Accommodation (hotels, pensions, youth hostel, dortoirs - Chalet en Plein Air Tel: (026) 83 23 50 and Club Alpin Tel: (026) 83 11 61), camping, restaurants, shops, banks, PTT, bus link with Orsières and Martigny. Office du Tourisme, 1938 Champex-Lac (Tel: (026) 83 12 27)*

Arriving in Champex late in the afternoon we sought dortoir accommodation and were soon booked in, with surprisingly up-market comfortable beds in a dormitory with curtains dividing the room to allow a degree of privacy not normally experienced in such places. I went for a shower and came out at the same time as a Dutchman whom we'd met the previous evening in Trient. We both had wet towels and socks to dry so went onto the balcony outside our room to hang them out overnight. As we stood there, suddenly the balcony floor gave way and crashed onto the

Champex (Photo: Walt Unsworth)

pavement, leaving the Dutchman and me hanging from the rail high above the street. It seemed a strange way to spend an evening, after the crossing of the Fenêtre d'Arpette, and we were wondering how we could swing back into our room in safety when a shout from below caught our attention. It was a German trekker who'd also been in Trient the previous night. 'This looks good', he called, waving his camera. 'Hold it there, I would like a photo of this'.

✳ ✳ ✳

Places or Features of Interest Along the Way:

1. **TOUR OF MONT BLANC:** This classic, scenically spectacular walk makes a circuit of the Mont Blanc massif by way of the seven valleys that surround it. The TMB has numerous *Variantes*, but the standard route is some 190 kilometres long and takes about 10 days to complete. With some justification it is one of the most popular of all long-distance routes in Europe. See *The Tour of Mont Blanc by Andrew Harper* (Cicerone Press).

2. CHAMPEX: Often known as Champex-Lac to emphasise its lakeside position, this modest-sized village has been developed as an all-year resort. During the summer there's swimming in a heated pool, boating and fishing in the lake. The alpine garden (*Jardin alpin Florealpe*) above the village on the hillside to the north (on the Tour de Champex) contains more than 4000 plants and is generally reckoned to be the finest collection in Switzerland. Entrance is free, and the garden is open to the public from 10-12.00 daily except Sundays and Mondays.

The Col de Balme. In the background is the huge bulk of Mont Blanc and left, the Aiguilles Verte and Dru (Stage 2).
(Walt Unsworth)

Sous la Le, a village on the walk from Champex to Sembrancher (Stage 4)

The Combin massif seen from above the Cabane du Mont Fort (Stage 5)

ALTERNATIVE STAGE 3:
TRIENT - COL de la FORCLAZ - BOVINE - CHAMPEX

Distance:	16 kilometres	
Time:	5½ hours	
Start altitude:	1279m	*High point:* Bovine 1987m
Height gain:	876m	*Height loss:* 657m
Map:	L.S. 5003 Mont Blanc - Grand Combin 1:50,000	
Accommodation:	La Forclaz (45 mins) - hotel, dortoir	
	Bovine (2½hrs) - dortoir	
	Champex - hotels, pensions, youth hostel,	
	dortoirs, camping	
Transport options:	Postbus (Trient-La Forclaz-Martigny)	
	Train (Martigny-Orsières)	
	Bus (Orsières-Champex)	

This route is the bad-weather alternative to the more demanding Fenêtre d'Arpette crossing, but it should not be assumed that it is an uninteresting walk. Far from it. It's a green and pleasant way, among forest and pasture and with good views down into the Rhône valley and across to the Bernese Alps that rise on the northern side. Since this is the path of the main TMB (the Fenêtre route is a Variante) it is waymarked and well-used.

It's interesting to note that when Whymper crossed the Col de la Forclaz in 1864 he was constantly bothered by 'parasitic children' who pestered him and other travellers on the road. "These children swarm there like maggots in a rotten cheese," he wrote. "They carry baskets of fruit with which to plague the weary tourist. They flit around him like flies; they thrust the fruit in his face; they pester him with their pertinacity. Beware of them! - touch not their fruit...It is to no purpose to be angry; it is like flapping wasps - they only buzz more".

Such problems are hardly likely to face the walker on the Chamonix-Zermatt route today!

* * *

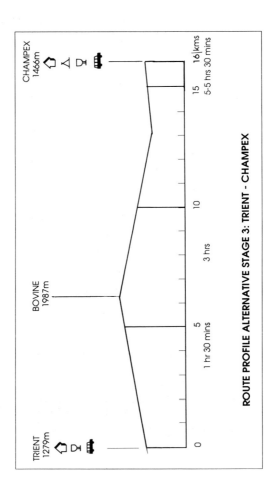

ROUTE PROFILE ALTERNATIVE STAGE 3: TRIENT - CHAMPEX

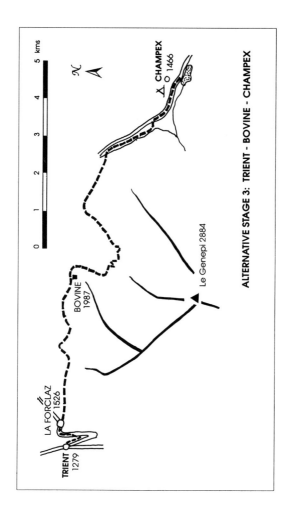

ALTERNATIVE STAGE 3: TRIENT - BOVINE - CHAMPEX

Take the path out of Trient which slants up the hillside to the east of the village and makes a short-cut of the Forclaz road, so to gain the pass at the clutch of buildings of **LA FORCLAZ** (1526m 45 mins *accommodation - Hotel du Col de la Forclaz; bedrooms and dortoir Tel: (026) 22 26 88 - refreshments, shop).*

The Bovine path begins on the right-hand side of the road almost opposite the hotel. It makes a rising traverse of the forested slopes, steeply in places, with views north to the Rhône valley seen through a 'V' of converging hillsides. Cross a high spur and slope down to the alp buildings of **BOVINE** (1987m 2$^{1/}$2hrs *accommodation, refreshments*) in an open pasture.

Continue round the hillside, soon veering south on a regular contour before dropping steeply into a combe, then crossing the rough pastures of **LA JURE** (1660m). Soon after join a track through forest, reaching **PLAN de L'AU** (1330m). Leave the track here and continue ahead on a path that enters the forest again, climbs among trees (a narrow trail), then veers left on a more level course. This may be a little overgrown. It leads to a dirt road that eventually disgorges onto a metalled road. Bear right and walk along it into **CHAMPEX**.

CHAMPEX (1466m 5^1/2 hours) *Accommodation (hotels, pensions, youth hostel, dortoirs - Chalet en Plein Air Tel: (026) 83 23 50 and Club Alpin Tel: (026) 83 11 61), camping, restaurants, shops, banks, PTT, bus link with Orsières and Martigny. Office du Tourisme, 1938 Champex-Lac (Tel: (026) 83 12 27)*

STAGE 4:
CHAMPEX - SEMBRANCHER - LE CHÂBLE

Distance:	13 kilometres	
Time:	4½ hours	
Start altitude:	1466m	*Low point*: Sembrancher 717m
Height loss:	749m	*Height gain*: 104 m
Map:	L.S. 5003 Mont Blanc - Grand Combin 1:50,000	
Accommodation:	Sembrancher (2 hours 45 mins) - hotels, camping	
	Le Châble - hotels, pension	
Transport options:	Bus (Champex-Orsières)	
	Train (Orsières-Sembrancher-Le Châble)	

A gentle downhill walk, followed by a pleasant valley stroll, this stage makes a good cushion between two rather strenuous days. Although there are no passes to cross, and no big glacier-hung mountains close at hand, it is by no means a dull day. Indeed, there is much to commend it, for the path takes you into an everyday working Switzerland. A Switzerland that rarely appears in tourist brochures, but which nevertheless is good to see. There are small farming communities along the way, patches of hillside being cultivated far from chocolate-box resorts, and with a general air of pastoral well-being.

If you were so inclined, Le Châble could be reached in a stiff morning's walk. But there'd be little to gain by rushing, for the onward route to Cabane du Mont Fort is too far to be achieved on top of this stage. Take the opportunity to enjoy a leisurely amble down to Sembrancher, and from there stroll into Val de Bagnes and make the most of your time..

Now at last, having left Champex, the route departs from that of the Tour of Mont Blanc and footpaths will be less busy.

* * *

Wander through Champex village heading south-east alongside the lake, and at the far end where the road forks at Hotel Grand

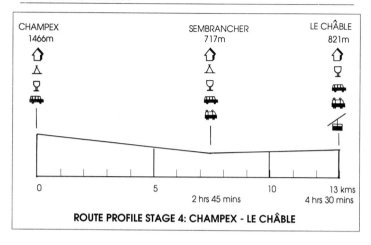

ROUTE PROFILE STAGE 4: CHAMPEX - LE CHÂBLE

Combin, take the left-hand branch. Rounding a dog-leg bend you come to the end of the road at Hotel Alpine. Ahead are two footpaths. Take the right-hand one descending into woods; it is signposted to Orsières and it loses height with a steady gradient to bring you to a track near the Champex-Orsières road. Go onto the road and walk downhill for 50 metres, then take a footpath on the left. This becomes a pleasant, easy track giving views into the Val d'Entremont below, and overlooking the village of Orsières.

The route brings you to a junction of tracks near the hamlet of **CHEZ LES REUSE** (1158m), but instead of dropping into the hamlet continue straight ahead on the path adopted by the [1] Tour des Combins. The track broadens and cuts into a cleft above a small gorge, then forks. Take the lower, right-hand branch which goes round pastureland, and you will come to another fork where this time you take the left-hand option. Before long come to a T junction of trails; bear left and 15 metres later slant off to the right on a grassy track signposted to Sous la Lé, La Garde and Sembrancher. The trail is waymarked and it brings you down to a gravel farm road above the small village of **SOUS LA LÉ** (marked as Souslalex, 1032m on the map).

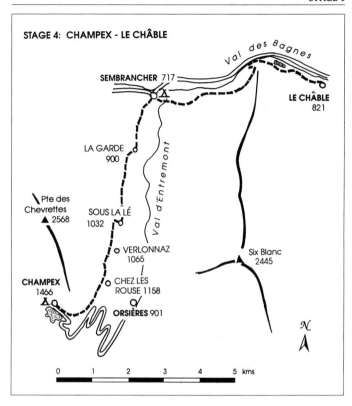

STAGE 4: CHAMPEX - LE CHÂBLE

Val des Bagnes

SEMBRANCHER 717

LE CHÂBLE
821

LA GARDE
900

Val d'Entremont

Pte des
Chevrettes
▲ 2568

SOUS LA LÉ
1032

○ VERLONNAZ
1065

Six Blanc
▲ 2445

CHAMPEX
1466

○ CHEZ LES
ROUSE 1158

ORSIÈRES 901

N

0   1   2   3   4   5 kms

Walk down to the village, and then head left at a water trough to go along a narrow street that leads to a junction of roads where you continue straight ahead, but instead of descending to a group of houses, take the left-hand track signposted to La Garde (45 minutes from here). Remain on the main, upper track when a choice is given, until a second track junction is reached immediately after crossing a hidden stream. Ignore that which cuts off left and continue ahead, now easing downhill among pastures to a junction of four tracks (**TETOU**). Go straight ahead on a path descending among trees and soon arrive in the village of **LA GARDE** (900m 2 hours 15 mins).

In the village pass a chapel on your right and walk along a street in the direction of St-Jean and Sembrancher, and down to a crosstracks where you go straight ahead, soon reaching a hairpin bend in a road. Once more continue ahead on a track again signposted to St-Jean and Sembrancher, following power lines. Between here and Sembrancher there are various footpath alternatives, with directions indicated at all route junctions. It is unnecessary to be precise, so simply follow whichever trail appeals. Any one will deliver you to Sembrancher, a village sitting at the junction of Val d'Entremont and Val de Bagnes.

SEMBRANCHER (717m 2 hours 45 mins *accommodation, camping, restaurants, shops, bank, PTT, Postbus and railway*) is a stone-walled village with an attractive little square, a good base for a walking holiday since it has access to two appealing valleys, and frequent public transport facilities.

Leave the village by walking up-valley on the road heading into Val d'Entremont, signposted (rather perversely) to Champex and Ferret. After 200 metres head left on a side road marked to Chamoille. Passing houses cross the river (La Drance d'Entremont) and go straight ahead where the road forks at **LES MOULINS** (729m). The narrow tarmac road goes between low-lying pastures and fields with encouraging views ahead. When you come to a fork near a small fenced building, take the right branch on what is now a track, and wander up into forest.

One or two junctions are met. The signs to follow are those for Le Châble, and, after a while, the track slopes down out of forest to an open space by a rifle range, winds downhill a little further, then follows the river (this time La Drance de Bagnes) upstream without diversion to **LE CHÂBLE**.

[2] **LE CHÂBLE** (821m 4½ hours) *Accommodation, restaurants, shops, banks, PTT, Postbus to Verbier, train to Martigny. Office du Tourisme, 1934 Le Châble (Tel: (026) 36 16 81) (Lower priced accommodation at: Les Alpes Garni Tel: (026) 36 14 65; Le Gietroz Tel: (026) 36 11 84; Escale Garni Tel: (026) 36 27 07; and Pension La Ruinette Tel: (026) 36 13 52) 'La Poste' (028) 36 11 69*

The village square at Sembrancher

Note: It is important to telephone ahead to Cabane de Prafleuri if you intend to have meals (end of Stage 6). Telephone (027) 81 11 56, or (027) 81 12 14. Alternatively, buy food before setting out on Stage 5.

* * *

Places or Features of Interest Along the Way:

1. **TOUR des COMBINS:** This is a walking tour of the Combins massif that begins and ends in Martigny in the Rhône valley. It takes 7-8 days to complete (total walking time about 48 hours) and leads first high above Val de Bagnes, down to Fionnay, then up to Cabane de Chanrion. From there the route strays into Italy before returning to Switzerland again and, crossing Col du Neve de la Rousse, descends through the Combe de l'A to Orsières. Up then to Champex and down to Martigny on the Rhône. (See *The Valais*, (Kev Reynolds) a walking guide in the same series as the present guidebook.)

2. **LE CHÂBLE:** This close-built village on the left bank of the Drance de Bagnes has some attractive corners and much neat pastoral countryside behind it. Whilst the main valley road is busy with tourist traffic by day, Le Châble escapes the worst of it and makes a convenient overnight resting place before tackling the steep uphill climb to Cabane du Mont Fort.

LE CHÂBLE - CLAMBIN - CABANE du MONT FORT

Distance:	9 kilometres
Time:	6-6¹/₂ hours
Start altitude:	821m *High point:* Cabane du Mont Fort 2457m
Height gain:	1636m
Map:	L.S. 5003 Mont Blanc - Grand Combin 1:50,000
Accommodation:	Cabane du Mont Fort - SAC refuge
Transport options:	Postbus (Le Châble-Verbier)
	Cableway (Verbier-Les Ruinettes)
	Cableway (Le Châble-Verbier-Les Ruinettes)

A first glance at the map gives little indication that a walking route can be made between Val de Bagnes and Cabane du Mont Fort without either extensive use of the steeply twisting road to Verbier, or the lengthy zig-zag road from Lourtier through Sarreyer.

But there is a route, and a delightful one at that. It is a combination of narrow lanes, tracks and footpaths - often steeply climbing, but always interesting. There are some fine villages, an attractive chapel, long forest sections with welcome shade on a hot day, high pastures and some truly magnificent views. With so much height to gain it is advisable to make an early start, take your time and enjoy everything the ascent has to offer. But it is also advisable to check-in at the refuge in good time to ensure bed-space if you are tackling the route in high season. (As with other overnight accommodation on the Chamonix-Zermatt walk, in high season it is probably safer to telephone your reservation ahead. The telephone number for the Mont Fort hut is given at the end of the route details.)

This route avoids Verbier altogether in an effort to remain as far from mechanisation as possible. It's impossible to escape all sign of the downhill ski industry here, however, for Verbier and its surrounding hillsides offer a winter paradise for the skier, and an abundance of lifts and cableways

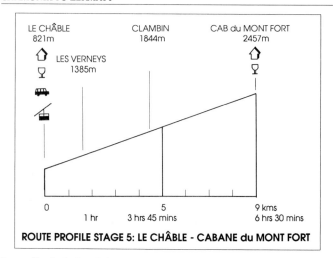

ROUTE PROFILE STAGE 5: LE CHÂBLE - CABANE du MONT FORT

have effectively laced the mountains like an old-fashioned corset. Whilst one deplores such desecration, thanks must be offered that a wholesale sacrifice has not been made to the transitory thrill of downhill skiing, that there are still ways for the wanderer to escape and that even here, paths may be found that ignore pylons and cables, and rejoice in vistas of sheer enchantment.

It is on this stage that the Grand Combin begins to exert its influence. This great snowy massif dominates the Val de Bagnes (and, to an extent, Val d'Entremont too). It's the first of the 4000 metre mountains of the Pennine Alps, an attractive, substantial block that cultivates a number of glaciers and whose presence is recognised for several days yet to come. Although the walk does not stray to it, the Combin nevertheless imposes its personality on the Haute Route trekker with its beauty and size. Since leaving Mont Blanc (whose bulk was always behind you), the Combin massif is the first on the walk to impress with such authority and grace.

From Le Châble cross the river and bear left. (The route is initially part of the Tour des Villages, and is waymarked with yellow diamonds or stripes outlined with black.) Head to the right past
60

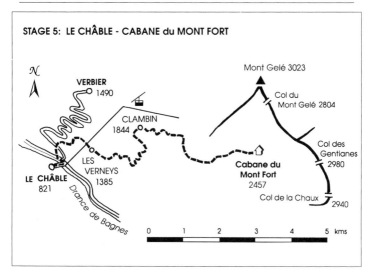

STAGE 5: LE CHÂBLE - CABANE du MONT FORT

Café-Restaurant La Ruinette and follow waymarks up through the village, passing houses and dark timber granaries, some of which are perched on staddle stones, along narrow streets. In 10 minutes you will reach **COTTERG** (880m) where you bear right (signpost to Chapelle les Verneys) to continue with waymarks and signposts as your guide on a series of tracks and footpaths to **LA FONTENELLE**. As you come to this hamlet, dug into the steep hillside, take a narrow footpath breaking away beside a wooden cross (dated 1982) to edge alongside an orchard. A track soon takes you round the hillside heading south-east, and eventually brings you to the small but elegant white chapel and few buildings of **LES VERNEYS** (1385m 1 hour *water supply, public toilet*).

Continue along the track beyond the buildings, and you will soon come to a footpath leading uphill on the left above the track. This goes into forest, gaining height steeply at times, in order to cross a scoop in the mountainside. This 'scoop' opens to a combe higher up. The way goes over a stream and climbs on, but having gained a high point you then descend a few metres to a junction of paths (about 25 minutes from Les Verneys). Head to the left, rising again, still in forest. The path is signposted to Verbier and Les Ruinettes.

This trail rises quite steeply on the right-hand (south) side of what soon becomes a distinctive combe, and comes to a handful of timber buildings above which you cross a track/road and take an upper track veering left. This winds up in long loops to and fro, with waymarked footpath short-cuts.

The footpath leads up to a pair of wooden buildings and passes between them (**LA COMBE**). A few paces beyond the path forks. Take the lower option across the hillside combe, enter forest and continue to a footpath junction where you bear right on a rising trail signposted to Clambin and Les Ruinettes. (Straight ahead the path goes to Verbier.) From here to Clambin waymarks are red and blue. It's a steep ascent, but when you come out of forest to a small open patch of pasture, the rewards are given in full bounty - a wonderful view of the [1] Combin massif shining its snow and ice on the far side of Val de Bagnes. This is the first of many magnificent sightings, but the magic never fades.

Continue towards a stone-built chalet, but veer left before it and pass beside a timber chalet with [2] Verbier seen below to the left in a large grassy bowl. An easy grass path then brings you to a junction of tracks at **CLAMBIN** (1844m 3 hours 45 mins *refreshments*). Go right, then immediately left on a track signposted to Les Ruinettes and Cabane du Mont Fort, climbing towards another chalet. (Waymarks have again reverted to yellow and black.)

This track eases gently up to another junction (**HATAY** 1884m) where you bear right and a few paces later slant left uphill and come to a picnic/barbecue area marked as **LE HATTEY** (1960m *water supply*). Bear left at another path junction and continue climbing through woods, emerging at last to spectacular views of the Grand Combin, and the Mont Blanc massif beyond intervening ridges in the south-west.

On this upward path we came upon an elderly Swiss couple descending. They wore smiles as bright as their red shirts and were so obviously

*The path to the Cabin du Mont Fort with the
Grand Combin in the distance*

enjoying their day out that we stopped to speak and shared with them a love of the morning, of the near views and far, and talked briefly of other mountains and valleys, of huts and villages, of glaciers and snowfields and birdsong and the fragrance of the forest. In general feeding off each other's enthusiasm. Then the lady whispered that her husband could now only walk up the gentlest of hills - but he'd swallowed his pride and taken the occasional chair-lift or cable-car to enable him to reach loftier viewpoints from which he was happy to walk down. "Well," she confided, "he is 82."

With that my prejudices stacked against cableways in the mountains came crashing round me.

On coming to a track by a chair-lift (5 hours 15 mins from Le Châble) turn right along it. Before long this rises as a path, crosses another track then leads to the right along a dirt road for about 250 metres. Then a path goes up onto a small causeway beside a *bisse*. There are wonderful views still to Grand Combin and its neighbouring peaks and glaciers; views that draw you to them. Follow the *bisse* on an easy contour round the hillside to **CABANE du MONT FORT**. The hut stands on a bluff at a junction of trails with exceptionally fine views.

[3] **CABANE du MONT FORT** (2457m 6-6¹/₂ hours) *100 places, meals and drinks available when the guardian is in residence.*
Tel: (026) 38 13 84

*   *   *

Places or Features of Interest Along the Way:

1. **GRAND COMBIN**: This large and impressive mountain has several distinct summits over 4000 metres. Standing entirely in Switzerland the summit crown has a splay of ridges from which busy glacial systems pour down; the largest being the great Glacier de Corbassière which falls in a series of terraces to the north, and is the largest icefield in the Western Pennine Alps. (A fine close view of these icy terraces is to be had from Cabane de Pannossière, reached by a 4 hour walk from Fionnay.) Although several ascents were made of secondary peaks in the massif in 1857-58 in the mistaken belief that they were the highest, the actual summit of Grand Combin (4314m) was climbed on 30 July 1859 by C St C Deville, with the guides G, E & G Balleys and B Dorsaz.

2. **VERBIER**: One of the best-known ski resorts in the Alps, Verbier occupies a large natural basin of hillside high above the valley, a real sun-trap and an obvious site for development as a ski village since the amphitheatre that backs it holds plenty of snow and the slopes

are ideal for skiers of all standards. It has an over-abundance of mechanical lifts - 80 or so, if you take into account those of the neighbouring Val de Nendaz which is easily accessible from it. The original village has long been engulfed by a rash of chalets, hotels and apartments, but there are many footpaths leading from it that take the eager walker into scenes of peace and tranquility. (For further information contact: Office du Tourisme, 1936 Verbier Tel: (026) 31 62 22)

3. **CABANE du MONT FORT**: Owned by the Jaman Section of the Swiss Alpine Club, this hut is superbly placed on a grassy bluff due south of Mont Gelé. It is used extensively by ski-touring enthusiasts in the spring and there are several high passes easily reached from it, including Col du Mont Gelé, Col des Gentianes, Col de la Chaux and Col Termin. These are all crossed by walkers in summer. Unfortunately a lacing of cableways has devalued some of these passes in recent years, but others happily remain free from mechanisation. Views from the hut are splendid, with Grand Combin and Mont Blanc taking pride of place. Sunsets are magnificent from here. Because of its ease of access by cable-car, the hut is very busy - especially during the day when it is used as a refreshment stop for parties of walkers.

STAGE 6:
CABANE du MONT FORT - COL TERMIN -
COL de LOUVIE - COL de PRAFLEURI -
CABANE de PRAFLEURI

Distance:	13 kilometres	
Time:	5¹/₂-6 hours	
Start altitude:	2457m	*High point:* Col de Prafleuri 2965m
Height gain:	885m	*Height loss:* 740m
Map:	L.S. 5003 Mont Blanc - Grand Combin 1:50,000	
Accommodation:	Cabane de Prafleuri - mountain refuge (privately owned)	
Transport options:	Cable-car (La Chaux-Col des Gentianes-Tortin) and see Alternative Stage 6 for continuing route from there.	

For many years mountain walkers attempting to work out a traverse of the high country between Val de Bagnes and Val des Dix sought ways of avoiding the Grand Désert, the broad glacier that is draped down the northern flanks of Rosablanche. Alternative passes were tried, and long circuitous routes taken via the lower reaches of Val de Nendaz. And there are those today who opt for the Col du Mont Gelé - a relatively easy pass above Cabane du Mont Fort, offered as Alternative Stage 6 - rather than face a glacial crossing. But with the shrinking of alpine glaciers in general, and the Grand Désert in particular in this instance, the three passes of Termin, Louvie and Prafleuri become practical for most mountain walkers. The glacier is still there to be crossed (although it would be possible to descend farther down-valley to avoid the ice and glacial lake below it altogether), but at the point of crossing the icefield has a gentle angle and any crevasses that might exist should be detected and easily stepped across. (It is doubtful whether any occur now on this low, fairly level section - and none at all were seen on the crossing made in research for this guide.)

The stage is full of variety and with constantly changing views. At first there are vast panoramas, and as you wander on the high belvedere path to Col Termin, so the Combin massif dominates the scene and you should walk quietly and remain alert to the possibility of seeing ibex on or near the path. (This is a noted wildlife sanctuary.) Later you are faced with a bewildering landscape of dying glaciers, tumbled moraines and large areas of barren wilderness. But even in such landscapes the majesty of the mountains impresses itself; yet one grows convinced (if you ever needed convincing) that the 'everlasting hills' are everlasting only in the words of the poet. On this walk you are witness to the ceaseless toil of erosion. The mountains are dying, falling apart, and to wander through their scenes of destruction is a sobering experience.

Under normal summer conditions this stage should cause no undue problems, but in poor visibility, or under threat of storm, difficulties may arise on the stretch between Col de Louvie (2921m) and Col de Prafleuri (2965m) where there is no path other than a trail of cairns and paint flashes. Seek the advice of the guardian at Cabane du Mont Fort in case of uncertainty.

Note: *There are no opportunities for refreshment along this section of the route, so make a point of filling your water bottles before leaving the hut.*

See also *Alternative Stage 6 for a variation of the route, going over Col du Mont Gelé above the hut. This avoids a glacier crossing.*

✳   ✳   ✳

Descend north-east from Cabane du Mont Fort to the major junction of paths below the hut. Head to the right on a path marked 'Tour du Val de Bagnes et Combin'. In a few metres the path forks. Bear left ahead and you will shortly come down onto a track which you descend to the second hairpin bend. Leave the track here in favour of a footpath which will traverse the scree slope seen ahead. This is the *Sentier des Chamois*.

Beyond the screes the trail climbs at a steady gradient with beautiful views to enjoy. It becomes a fine belvedere of a path and is where you may well catch sight of ibex (*bouquetin* in French).

We were finding the path difficult to negotiate. Not that there were

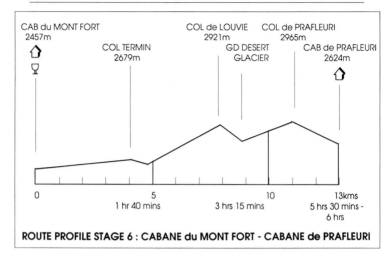

CAB du MONT FORT
2457m

COL TERMIN
2679m

COL de LOUVIE
2921m

COL de PRAFLEURI
2965m

GD DESERT
GLACIER

CAB de PRAFLEURI
2624m

0

5
1 hr 40 mins

10
3 hrs 15 mins

13kms
5 hrs 30 mins -
6 hrs

ROUTE PROFILE STAGE 6 : CABANE du MONT FORT - CABANE de PRAFLEURI

obstacles in the way, nor were conditions at all bad. Neither were we bothered by the steep slopes plunging to Val de Bagnes fifteen hundred metres below. Our problems arose from lack of concentration, for the glories of the Combin massif across the valley were so outstanding that our attention was being trapped by them - away from the first principle of safety on the path. I found it difficult to take my eyes off that gleaming mass that had conjured a streamer of cloud just below the summit, and was teasing us now as in a dance of the seven veils. The summit was clear, so were the lower slopes. But the midriff of the mountain was veiled. It was a tantalising view. Then, when I did correct my attention to review the way ahead, it was to spy a herd of twenty or so ibex moving unconcerned in the shadows just below the path. They were close, very close, and completely unbothered by our presence. I only cursed the shadows that effectively barred photography.

In a little over an hour from the hut you reach a path junction where a trail breaks off to descend. Ignore this and continue straight ahead to cross another scree slope, climb over a spur (fixed chains to safeguard the way in icy conditions), and continue round the mountainside on a narrow but easy path that nevertheless has some

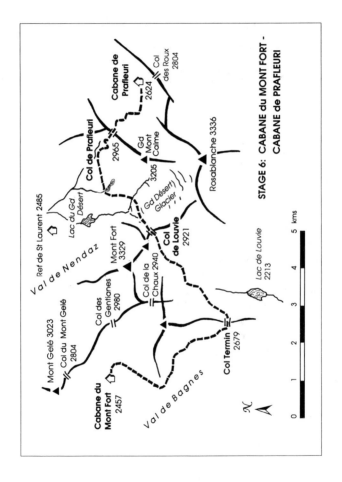

STAGE 6: CABANE du MONT FORT - CABANE de PRAFLEURI

exposed sections. Views remain magnificent; Grand Combin aloof across the valley, and the Val de Bagnes itself a very long way beneath the path. Views back to the north-west show the Dents du Midi in the distance.

The way then reaches the obvious saddle of **COL TERMIN** (2679m 1 hour 40 mins) in a shoulder of Bec Termin which rises to the north. From here a very wild landscape rises to north and east, with Mont Fort and [1] Rosablanche both casting out high ridges to confuse.

Descend on the east side for a few metres, then veer sharply left on the path signposted to Col de Louvie and Prafleuri. Steeply below lies Lac de Louvie, a tarn popular with anglers and walkers alike. (There is a refuge on its shore, and from a short distance to the south of the tarn one of the finest views in the Swiss Alps is to be enjoyed. It is worth remembering for a return visit to Val de Bagnes.) Fifteen minutes from the col another path breaks away and descends to the lake, but you continue on towards a wild-looking rocky cirque at the head of the Louvie valley. A rough boulder tip is crossed, but after this the path improves. Views remain impressive.

An hour from Col Termin you come to a path junction where the left-hand option heads for Col de la Chaux and Mont Fort. Ignore this and continue straight ahead, over a second boulder field and, skirting the left-hand side of a narrow stony valley (good waymarks and a clear path), you climb to gain the wild and rocky **COL de LOUVIE** (2921m 3 hours 15 mins).

A barren landscape greets you in the north-east; a wilderness of screes, moraine and the dying glacier spewing from Rosablanche. The Grand Désert is indeed well-named.

Descend towards the glacier following red and white paint marks. (Orange waymarks lead the way down to Refuge de St Laurent and the Val de Nendaz, and as the two routes diverge it is important to take the correct way in order to avoid unnecessary height loss.) Just before you reach the edge of the glacier there is a boulder with large waymarks painted on it, you will see on the far side of the ice a few continuing waymarks. A marker pole provides directional aid. Should visibility be poor, however, cross the glacier on a compass bearing of 72°. It should cause no problems in crossing (about 10 minutes), and on the eastern side you follow waymarks over moraine rubble, skirting little tarns and glacial ponds, crossing broad granite slabs and jumbled boulders. Waymarks are frequent, but in poor visibility it is absolutely essential not to lose sight of them. Take compass bearings if necessary.

Col de Prafleuri is seen at the head of what looks like a steep slope of scree. A small glacier flows down from Grand Mont Calme to one side of the pass, and the waymarked trail brings you to the edge of it where it is necessary to descend a short slope of ice (sometimes snow-covered) in order to continue to the foot of the pass. Descend with care.

The climb to the col may be found rather tiring as it involves working a way up a steepish slope of rough blocks and scattered rocks. So reach **COL de PRAFLEURI** (2965m 5 hours) to be greeted by a view south-east over a much-scarred and depressingly barren mountain bowl to Mont Blanc de Cheilon which dominates much of the route of Stage 7.

Descend the steep path winding down to a level stretch beneath the Glacier de Prafleuri; cross levelled gravel beds to a track where you bear right, soon leaving this on a waymarked footpath that drops to the left into a grim-looking valley where you have a first sighting of **CABANE de PRAFLEURI**. Waymarks lead straight to it.

[2] **CABANE de PRAFLEURI** (2624m 5¹/2-6 hours) *56 places, meals provided when booked in advance (tel: (027) 81 11 56, or (027) 81 12 14), small kitchen with all utensils provided , guardian in residence during the summer season. A simple, basic hut but with a welcoming guardian.*

* * *

Places or Features of Interest Along the Way:

1. **ROSABLANCHE**: This snow peak of 3336 metres offers easy ascent routes and a superb panorama from its summit - an exceptionally fine viewpoint from which to study larger peaks of

the main Pennine chain. It is popular as a skiing expedition in spring, and from the Prafleuri hut by walkers in summer (2 hours from the hut by way of the Prafleuri glacier). It was first climbed in September 1865.

2. **CABANE de PRAFLEURI:** Privately-owned, the hut was constructed in the mid-fifties when quarrying work began below the Prafleuri glacier as part of the Grande Dixence hydro-electric scheme. (It was used to house site workers in the early days.) Whilst it lacks any views of inspiration, it is particularly well-sited for walkers on the Chamonix-Zermatt route for immediately above it to the south is the easy Col des Roux which gives access to the Val des Dix. Ibex may be spied near the hut.

ALTERNATIVE STAGE 6:
CABANE du MONT FORT - COL du MONT GELÉ -
COL de PRAFLEURI - CABANE de PRAFLEURI

Distance:	17 kilometres	
Time:	8 hours	
Start altitude:	2457m	*High point:* Col de Prafleuri 2965m
Height gain:	1339m	*Height loss:* 1172m
Map:	L.S. 5003 Mont Blanc - Grand Combin 1:50,000 ·	
Accommodation:	Refuge St Laurent (4¹/₂ hours) - mountain refuge (Arpettaz Ski Club)	
	Cabane de Prafleuri - mountain refuge (privately-owned)	
Transport options:	None	

In order to avoid a crossing of the Grand Désert glacier, some Haute Route trekkers opt for the less-direct route which visits the upper Val de Nendaz and the dammed Lac de Cleuson on the way to Col de Prafleuri. However, snow patches often linger on the eastern side of Col du Mont Gelé and caution should be exercised, especially during the early part of the summer.

Val de Nendaz itself is a pleasant green valley whose pastures are rich in wild flowers. Cableways, erected primarily to service the ski industry, link the valley with Verbier's ski fields via Col de Chassoure (north of Mont Gelé) and the Col des Gentianes/Mont Fort/La Chaux complex above Cabane du Mont Fort. But elsewhere Val de Nendaz has a pastoral atmosphere, while above the Lac de Cleuson lies that intermediate region where vegetation is gradually exchanged for the barren uplands scoured by recently-lost ice sheets.

❋   ❋   ❋

The path to Col du Mont Gelé is not signposted, but north of the Mont Fort hut a narrow trail leads up into an obvious grassy bowl to the left of a jumble of rocks with the obvious col seen in the ridge

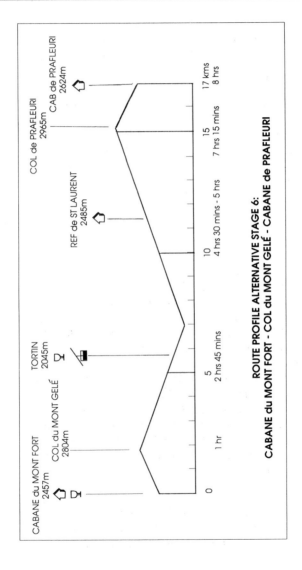

ROUTE PROFILE ALTERNATIVE STAGE 6:
CABANE du MONT FORT - COL du MONT GELÉ - CABANE de PRAFLEURI

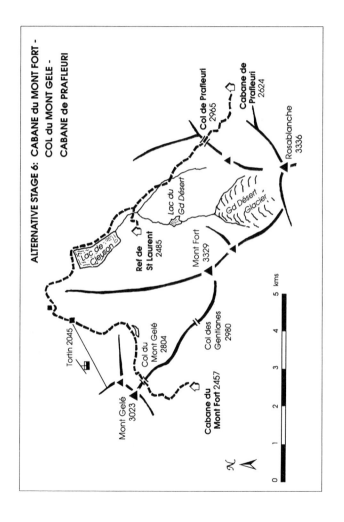

ALTERNATIVE STAGE 6: CABANE du MONT FORT -
COL du MONT GELE -
CABANE de PRAFLEURI

Col de Prafleuri
2965

Cabane de
Prafleuri
2624

Rosablanche
3336

Lac du
Gd Désert

Gd Désert
Glacier

Lac de
Cleuson

Ref de
St Laurent
2485

Mont Fort
3329

Tortin 2045

Col du
Mont Gelé
2804

Col des
Gentianes
2980

Mont Gelé
3023

Cabane du
Mont Fort 2457

0   1   2   3   4   5   kms

N

above. As you proceed through the bowl, so the path becomes more distinct. There are waymarks and one or two marker posts and the poor grass covering soon loses out to a stony waste. The climb to the pass is up rocky terrain, but the ascent is accomplished without difficulty. (There may be snow patches lying on the approach to the pass, as well as on the eastern side.)

COL du MONT GELÉ (2804m 1 hour) lies to the south-east of its eponymous peak. (For those inclined, this may be reached in 30 minutes from the col - an excellent viewpoint.) Views from the col are fine down to Val de Bagnes in one direction, Val de Nendaz in the other. Over the col snow banks are often found. Head to the right (east) for a short distance (to about the 'G' of Gelé on the map), then go north with due care (an ice-axe would be helpful in some conditions) down a snow slope to find a path which heads off to the right descending towards a small tarn. Pass above this tarn on its northern side, then round a spur sloping down from Mont Gelé. The path continues along hillsides flanking a small tributary valley that feeds Val de Nendaz, and you come to the cable-car station at **TORTIN** (2045m 2 hours 45 mins *refreshments*).

From the alp below the cable-car station take the jeep track which cuts across to the right-hand side of the valley. When it forks do not follow the north-bound track to the lower valley and hamlet of Super Nendaz, but continue round a wooded spur of L'Arpette and head south towards the barrage of Lac de Cleuson. Follow the broad track that heads along the eastern side of the lake and continue beyond it to a signposted junction of trails.

Note: If you require overnight accommodation continue ahead and cross the stream on a wooden footbridge, then climb round in easy loops up to **REFUGE de ST LAURENT** (2485m 4¹/₂-5 hours *50 spaces, guardian in residence in summer, self-catering facilities. Take your own food*.) Should you decide to break the journey here, it might be worth taking Alternative Route 7 from Cabane de Prafleuri (which will be reached in a morning's walk from here) as far as Cabane des Dix for your next night's accommodation.

For the Col de Prafleuri bear left at the junction, then head to the right (south) at the next junction a little higher. Continue upvalley, crossing and recrossing the stream where necessary, rising south-eastwards with the Grand Mont Calme ridge directly ahead. Col de Prafleuri lies just below the junction of the Mont Calme ridge and that of the Monts Rosets which walls the upper valley to the left. To the right of the col a small glacier comes down from Grand Mont Calme.

Waymarks and sections of path lead you to a clutter of rocks over which the final ascent is made. So to gain **COL de PRAFLEURI** (2965m 7 hours 15 mins) with Rosablanche seen off to the right (south) and Mont Blanc de Cheilon ahead far beyond an intervening ridge. Tomorrow's route leads almost to that great triangular wedge.

The descent to the hut will take about 50 minutes from here. The path winds down quite steeply to reach a level stretch beneath the Glacier de Prafleuri. Cross levelled gravel beds (waymarks) to a track where you turn right, soon leaving this on a waymarked path that drops down to the left into a sorry-looking narrow valley where you catch sight at last of the **CABANE de PRAFLEURI**. Waymarks lead straight to it.

CABANE de PRAFLEURI (2624m 8 hours) *56 places, meals provided if booked in advance (tel: (027) 81 11 56, or (027) 81 12 14), guardian in residence during the summer. All cooking and eating utensils provided, but no food. A basic hut, privately-owned.*

STAGE 7:
CABANE de PRAFLEURI - COL des ROUX -
COL de RIEDMATTEN - AROLLA

Distance:	16 kilometres
Time:	6¹/₂ hours
Start altitude:	2624m *High point:* Col de Riedmatten 2919m
Height gain:	735m *Height loss:* 1361m
Map:	L.S. 5003 Mont Blanc - Grand Combin 1:50,000
Accommodation:	Arolla - hotels, dortoir, camping
Transport options:	Bus (Le Chargeur-Vex)
	Postbus (Vex-Arolla)

The walk which leads from the rather depressing, man-savaged Prafleuri glen to Arolla is a true delight. Given fine weather conditions the views on this stage will be among the very best of them all. There's the surprise vision that greets you on arrival at the first col of the day (Col des Roux), for you emerge from the constrictions of morning shadow to the incredible sight of the Val des Dix spread before you - a five kilometre lake, green pastures and big mountains. Best of all these mountains is the great triangular-shaped Mont Blanc de Cheilon; but it has its handsome neighbours too, and as the day progresses so you draw closer to them, crossing Col de Riedmatten to descend beside Pigne d'Arolla, then below Mont Collon. Col de Riedmatten is in itself a revelation, a rocky cleft in the ridge of the Monts Rouges, and from it you have a first view of the Matterhorn far off. (Make the most of it, for you'll not see it again after you reach Zinal on Stage 11!)

Despite the fact that you have two passes to cross, this stage is not unduly taxing, for by now you should be well into your stride and pacing the days in comfort. Only the last pull up to Col de Riedmatten may be found a little tiring, but once on the pass the beauty of the scene before you will throw that momentary weariness into perspective.

There's no opportunity for refreshment along this route until you arrive in Arolla, so make sure your water bottle is full before setting out from the hut.

Note: *Alternative Stage 7 described below also makes a very fine day out with the opportunity to break the walk with an overnight spent in Cabane des Dix, which is dramatically situated beneath the great north face of Mont Blanc de Cheilon. Both routes offered have much to commend them, but the Col de Riedmatten crossing is the more direct.*

*   *   *

On leaving Cabane de Prafleuri walk upvalley for about 50 metres, then bear left (waymarking on rocks) to Col des Roux, an obvious pass just to the south of the hut and only 180 metres above it. The way to the col is by way of a slope of boulders and rocks, and as you gain height so a proper path is followed in easy zig-zags. In fact the ascent is achieved quickly and a lot more easily than might be imagined from first glance below, and you come onto **COL des ROUX** (2804m 20 mins) to be rewarded with a view almost guaranteed to stop you in your tracks.

Note: An alternative to the crossing of Col des Roux (in case of bad weather) is to go down-valley from the hut following the track on the right-hand side of the stream. This becomes a path which, rounding a rocky corner, overlooks the huge dam of [1]Le Chargeur at the northern end of Lac des Dix. The descent from hut to dam early in the season may be bothered with one or two snow chutes. If this is the case, take great care when crossing them, for a slip could be serious. On reaching the dam bear right and follow the track heading along the west side of the lake. This goes through several tunnels, the first being the longest and darkest. A switch at the entrance gives five minutes of light, which is sufficient time to get through. Follow the track to the far end of the lake where you join the main route described.

The path forks on the saddle of Col des Roux. Go straight over to the south side and descend on a continuing trail that brings you to more boulders, but then becomes easier under foot. The path veers south-westward into the gentle pastures cupping a shallow valley below

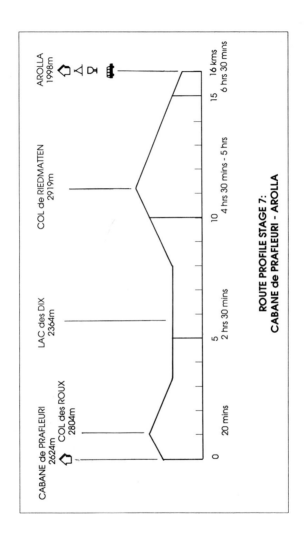

ROUTE PROFILE STAGE 7:
CABANE de PRAFLEURI - AROLLA

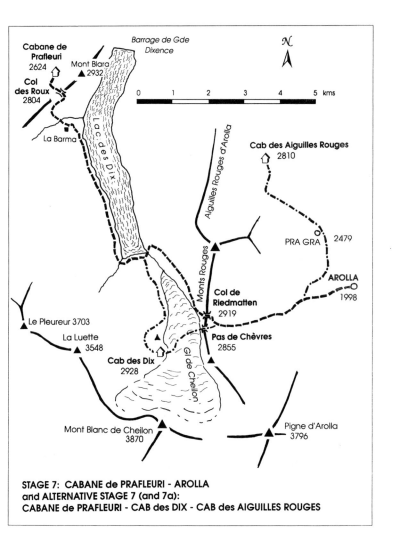

**STAGE 7: CABANE de PRAFLEURI - AROLLA
and ALTERNATIVE STAGE 7 (and 7a):
CABANE de PRAFLEURI - CAB des DIX - CAB des AIGUILLES ROUGES**

Descending from the Col des Roux into the Val des Dix.
In the distance is the Pigne d'Arolla (left)
and Mt Blanc de Cheilon (right)

the Glacier des Ecoulaies that is draped like a napkin down the breast of Le Parrain. Heading towards a lone farm building (unnamed on the map, but marked as 2575m), you swing away to the left in order to cross a stream, then ease round the hillside and come to the stone-built **LA BARMA** (2458m). Immediately before this head to the left on a descending path to join the lakeside track where you bear right.

The walk upvalley alongside the lake is a delightful one with little effort required. You can swing along with all your senses alert to the wonders of the day, with marmots whistling from the trackside pastures, the clang of cowbells matching your stride. There are signs warning of rockfall, streams spilling down the hillsides, and a wondrous snowgleam topping peaks ahead.

At the southern end of Lac des Dix you come to a metal suspension footbridge that crosses the south-eastern inlet. It's a slender bridge but a safe one, yet since you can see through the metal grid pattern to the water below, it might give those who suffer vertigo an uneasy moment! On the far side a steel staircase leads to a small works building and a narrow path heads uphill from it.

This path initially takes you through a very flowery patch (edelweiss and field gentians) and then enters a stony valley carved by the Cheilon glacier. This valley grows wider as you head south, but on entering, it is narrow and somewhat littered with boulders. The path works its way along the left-hand side, over boulder fields and across streams, then zig-zags to gain height. All the time [2] Mont Blanc de Cheilon gleams ahead, its glacier and long trough of moraine sweeping through the valley floor, creating new landscapes for some future generation of Haute Route walkers to wander through.

Some far-off day pastures of lush grass will no doubt carpet this valley like so many farther down. There'll be flowers sparkling in spring and early summer, cattle, perhaps, grazing where today only moraine grit and stone and dirty glacial ice spread their stark outlines. The mountains too will look somewhat different, and Mont Blanc de Cheilon will have lost the upper glaciers that at present drape its south, east and western flanks, and it may then take on a replica appearance of the Matterhorn, carved into a smooth-sided pinnacle by that very ice - as its north face has already been planed by the disappearing glacier of Cheilon.

After a fairly lengthy level stretch the path suddenly swings left (eastward) and climbs steeply to gain the narrow notch of **COL de RIEDMATTEN** (2919m 4$^{1}/_{2}$-5 hours) and a window onto a new world.

Trading shadows for sunshine on my first crossing of Col de Riedmatten we gained that rocky cleft and light suddenly flooded ahead, washing a delectable land of snow, ice, rock and a distant slope of grass. Below, the ridge fell into a basin of mountain-rejected debris, but our eyes were uninterested in any of this, for our attention was held by the crest of Pigne d'Arolla, by the great iced gateau of Mont Collon, by the sharp stiletto blade of the Matterhorn's upper reaches far off, by a vast wall of rock notable for the little spire of the Aiguille de la Tsa projecting from it, and by the snow-wrapped Dent Blanche on the far side of that wall.

We'd had the path to ourselves, but within moments of our arrival on the col a middle-aged German couple arrived too, having come up from Arolla. Together we shared an enthusiasm for this magical place and helped each other identify peaks on a serrated horizon. With the aid of their powerful binoculars we could make out the glitter of one or two remote huts dazzling in the sun on mountains far-off. Ah, the world would be grand from those distant lodgings too, yet I harboured no twinge of longing for the Col de Riedmatten gave as much grandeur as I could take for now.

Note: For an even broader view than may be gained from the col, follow the narrow trail which bears left onto the ridge, but take care as it requires a little scrambling in places. It is only necessary to go a short distance to win a huge panorama.

Descending to the east the path is clearly defined, although rather steep at first. It leads into an undulating grassy bowl where it veers to the right and joins another path that comes down from Pas de Chèvres (crossed on Alternative Stage 7). Now heading to the left (east) the path, clear and undemanding, takes you easily towards Arolla. Mont Collon disappears from view, but [3] Pigne d'Arolla

The Pigne d'Arolla seen from the descent to Arolla

grows in stature on the right with the long Tsijiore Nouve glacier
carving its way from the heights in a deep trench behind a grass-
covered wall of moraine. Then, as you approach Arolla, so [(4)] Mont
Collon reappears like an island in a sea of ice.

The way divides two or three times, but you simply follow the
waymarked trail down to **AROLLA**.

[(5)] **AROLLA** (1998m 6¹/₂ hours) *Accommodation (hotels, pension, dortoir
- Hotel de la Tsa 15 mins below Arolla) Tel: (027) 83 4 06 Other dortoir
accommodation at Hotel du Glacier (027) 83 12 18. Lower priced hotels:
Hotel de la Poste Tel: (027) 83 11 64; Hotel du Pigne d'Arolla Tel: (027)
83 11 65; Hotel du Glacier Tel: (027) 83 12 18), room to rent at the village
shop opposite the Post Office, camping, restaurants, shops, PTT, Postbus
link with Les Haudères and Evolène. Further information from :
Office du Tourisme, 1961 Arolla Tel: (027) 83 10 83*

* * *

Places or Features of Interest Along the Way:

1. **LE CHARGEUR**: Otherwise known as the Grande Dixence, the huge dam at the northern end of Lac des Dix is a stupendous piece of engineering, and at 284 metres is claimed to be the highest barrage in the world. From its base to the crest of the dam it stands twice as tall, with twice the volume of the largest of Egypt's pyramids. It consists of 5,960,000 cubic metres of concrete and holds back some 400 million cubic metres of water. The dam was built in 1965.

2. **MONT BLANC de CHEILON**: This shapely mountain, 3870 metres high, dominates the Val des Dix and towers over the Cabane des Dix which serves it. Generally reckoned to be the finest peak in the Arolla district for rock and ice routes, it received its first ascent in September 1865 by the west-north-west flank which is reached from the Col de Cheilon. (The usual route today and the one most used in descent.)

3. **PIGNE d'AROLLA**: An easy snow mountain that neighbours Mont Blanc de Cheilon to the east, the Pigne is often ascended by ski mountaineers during a spring traverse of the classic *Haute Route*. An outstanding viewpoint, in one vast panorama most of the mountains of the Pennine Alps that feature in the Chamonix-Zermatt route can be seen; as too can the chain of the Bernese Alps. The Grand Paradis and the Graians are also visible, and it has been claimed that the Mediterranean can be seen from the summit on a clear day. The first ascent was made by A W Moore, H Walker and their guide J Anderegg in July 1865. Its height is 3796 metres; a distinctive peak recognised from afar.

4. **MONT COLLON**: More than any other, Mont Collon is the dominant feature of the Arolla valley (the upper south-western spur of Val d'Hérens). Despite its modest altitude (3637m), the rocky buttresses, snow domes and its apparent bulk give this mountain an imposing stature out of all proportion to its true size. Glaciers flow round its east and west flanks like icy callipers,

effectively giving Mont Collon the appearance of an island peak, but to the south it is attached to the higher L'Evêque by way of the Col de la Mitre. Mont Collon was first climbed by G E Foster with H Baumann and J Kronig in 1867. There are several routes of varying grades adorning its face, pillars and ridges today.

5. **AROLLA**: This small mountaineering centre was one of the first to be 'adopted' by the British. In his book *The Alps*, R L G Irving says: "...at Arolla is the nearest thing to an imperial possession which England has in the Alps, an English church." The village is steadily expanding, and there are one or two ski tows adorning the meadows (probably the greatest single threat - after the work of hydro-engineers - to the pastoral nature of any alpine village). But in spite of this Arolla remains one of the smallest villages on the Walker's Haute Route, and one with as fine a collection of surrounding mountains as you could wish to find. As the base for a mountaineer's first alpine season, Arolla could hardly be bettered, while it also makes a very fine walking centre. (See *The Valais*, (Kev Reynolds) a walking guide also published by Cicerone Press, for details.)

Mont Collon forms a splendid head to the Arolla valley. To its right is L'Évêque (Photo: Walt Unsworth) 87

ALTERNATIVE STAGE 7:
CABANE de PRAFLEURI - COL des ROUX - CABANE des DIX

Distance:	11 kilometres	
Time:	4-4$^{1/2}$ hours	
Start altitude:	2624m	*High point:* Cabane des Dix 2928m
Height gain:	744m	*Height loss:* 440m
Map:	L.S. 5003 Mont BLanc - Grand Combin 1:50,000	
Accommodation:	Cabane des Dix - SAC refuge	
Transport options:	None	

This alternative to the main route described above has much to commend it, and is particularly useful for walkers who crossed Col du Mont Gelé above Cabane du Mont Fort and spent a subsequent night in Refuge de St Laurent. By adopting this route, however, a glacier must be crossed when leaving Cabane des Dix. The glacier in question has a route marked over it, is heavily used and should cause no disquiet. (Crevasses are virtually non existent on the traverse route.)

The first part of the walk is the same as that taken on Stage 7, but departs from it at the southern end of Lac des Dix. From here a path leads along the left bank moraine of the Cheilon glacier, climbs over a shoulder of the rock promontory called the Tête Noire and drops below the hut.

Cabane des Dix enjoys a superb view onto the north face of Mont Blanc de Cheilon, and occupies a truly spectacular site. It is, however, an extremely busy hut and all intending to use it in high season (or at weekends just out of season) are urged to telephone their reservation in advance.

* * *

Follow route directions as for Stage 7 as far as the southern end of Lac des Dix (2$^{1/2}$ hours). About 50 metres before the metal

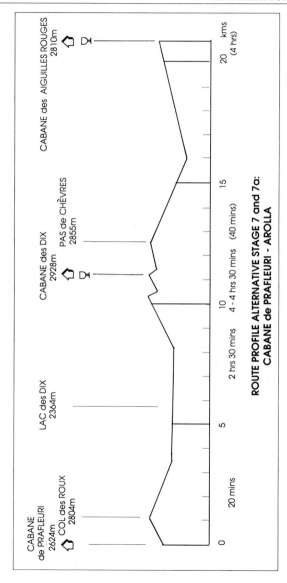

CABANE des AIGUILLES ROUGES 2810m

CABANE des DIX 2928m

PAS de CHÈVRES 2855m

LAC des DIX 2364m

CABANE de PRAFLEURI 2624m

COL des ROUX 2804m

ROUTE PROFILE ALTERNATIVE STAGE 7 and 7a:
CABANE de PRAFLEURI - AROLLA

20 mins   2 hrs 30 mins   4 - 4 hrs 30 mins   (40 mins)   (4 hrs)

0   5   10   15   20   kms

*The towering north face of Mont Blanc de Cheilon
dominates the Dix hut (Photo: Brian Evans)*

footbridge at the end of the track, head off to the right on a path that
climbs steeply and is signposted to Cabane des Dix.

At first the climb is quite steep, but it soon eases as you gain the
crest of a lateral moraine of the fast-receding Glacier de Cheilon. The
path is clear and the views ever-interesting, and as you make
progress along the moraine, so you can see the deep col of Pas de
Chèvres (the continuation route from the hut) on the far side of the
glacier.

Towards the end of the moraine the path forks. The left-hand
(continuing) route drops to the glacier to skirt the Tête Noire, but the
right-hand option is the one recommended. This descends a little,
then rises over grass slopes and onto screes by which you gain the
north-west shoulder of the Tête Noire which hides not only Mont
Blanc de Cheilon, but also the Cabane des Dix.

As you rise towards the saddle on this shoulder, a wonderful
panorama is seen off to the left (east). Far beyond the ridge of the

Monts Rouges a great jagged collection of peaks holds your attention. In that collection is the Matterhorn, whose profile from here is quite different from that normally seen from Zermatt. It appears as a distant stiletto with a marked shelf projecting to the south just beneath the summit. Then, when you gain the saddle, the vast pyramid of the north face of Mont Blanc de Cheilon soars in front of you, while below the hut can be seen perched on top of a rocky knoll. The path winds down into a glacial plain, crosses a stream or two, then strikes directly up the slope to reach the **CABANE des DIX**.

CABANE des DIX (2928m 4-4¹/₂ hours) *145 places, restaurant service, guardian in residence from mid March to mid September. Tel: (027) 81 15 23. Owned by the Monte Rosa section of the Swiss Alpine Club, this refuge is one of the busiest in the Alps and is patronised by walkers, climbers and ski-tourers alike.*

La Barma, Stage 7 and Alternative Stage 7

ALTERNATIVE STAGE 7a:
CABANE des DIX - PAS de CHÈVRES -
CABANE des AIGUILLES ROUGES/AROLLA

Distance:	10 kilometres (6 kms to Arolla)
Time:	4 hours (2½ hours to Arolla)
Start altitude:	2928m *High point:* Cabane des Dix 2928m
Height loss:	540m *Height gain:* 428m (30m)
	(957m to Arolla)
Map:	L.S. 5003 Mont Blanc - Grand Combin 1:50,000
Accommodation:	Cabane des Aiguilles Rouges - SAC refuge
	Arolla - hotels, pensions, dortoir, camping
Transport options:	None
Profile &Sketchmap:	Page 89 and page 81

The walk to Cabane des Aiguilles Rouges maintains the intrinsic character of the high route and the trekker opting for this gains by visiting one of the most attractive alps in Switzerland (Pra Gra), and also by enjoying spectacular views from the hut across the Arolla valley to its steep eastern wall. What is missed, of course, is a visit to Arolla itself.

Cabane des Aiguilles Rouges is situated in a somewhat barren rocky landscape immediately below the crusted ridge after which it is named. The aiguilles are not seen in their full grandeur from the hut, however, due to foreshortening, but they will be viewed in all their jagged glory on the way to Col de Torrent on Stage 9, and also from one or two passes further east.

There will be no opportunities for refreshment between the two huts, so fill water bottles before setting out.

* * *

On leaving Cabane des Dix descend the knoll on a clear path that winds leftwards (south) to the edge of the rubble-strewn Glacier de Cheilon, and then head north-east across it. Marker poles and cairns

The long ladders at the Pas de Chèvres
(Photo: Brian Evans)

direct the way; an easy crossing with practically no crevasses to worry about. You are soon on the eastern side where you wander up a slope of moraine and rocks on a partial path to reach the foot of a long, near-vertical ladder by which you overcome a steep slab to gain the col. There are two ladders, in fact, the first much longer than the second. Both are firmly attached to the rock face, but care should be exercised when carrying a large rucksack. One or two rungs are so close to the rock face that only the toes of your boots can gain purchase. (Some people may feel the need of a safety rope.)

So reach **PAS de CHÈVRES** (2855m 40 mins) where a very fine panorama is unfolded. This includes the Veisivi-Bertol wall above Arolla, with the delicate Aiguille de la Tsa projecting from it, and beyond that the top of Dent Blanche, summit cone of the Matterhorn, Mont Collon and many more. It's a col to relax on and enjoy before tearing yourself away to tackle the descent.

An easy path takes you down on the eastern side, at first quite steeply, into a bowl of rough grassland to join another path coming from the neighbouring Col de Riedmatten crossed on the main Stage 7 route. The walk down towards Arolla is taken sedately on a clear trail, much-trodden by walkers and climbers. On the right Pigne d'Arolla towers in a sweep of rock and ice, with the long Tsijiore Nouve glacier peeling down into a huge trough behind a grass-covered moraine wall. Views are consistently lovely.

When you reach a broad track breaking away to the left, leave the Arolla path and head off along it.

Note: For those aiming to visit Arolla, simply continue down the path. The way forks several times above the village, but all paths lead to it unless otherwise signposted. (See Stage 7 route description for further information.)

The track winds round the hillside, then you go up to the cluster of alp huts of **PRA GRA** (2479m), an idyllic setting of grey stone-roofed chalets, barns and cattle-byres on a green terrace.

Continue ahead (north-westward) on a clear, broad path across pastures and on to a wide plateau. The path now swings left into a wild region of boulder slopes and gravel beds with streams running through. Above this hang a small glacier and drapes of snow. Across the streams the way veers right to tackle more boulder slopes and scree, and on a short section a fixed chain gives reassurance when the path is icy. The final climb to the **CABANE des AIGUILLES ROUGES**, set on a rib of rock and scree, becomes a little steep, but is none too arduous.

CABANE des AIGUILLES ROUGES (2810m 4 hours) *80 places, meals and drinks available when the guardian is in residence in July and August. Owned by the Academic Alpine Club of Geneva.*

Note: For details of the continued walk to Lac Bleu, where you rejoin the main route, see Stage 8.

Arolla

STAGE 8:
AROLLA - LAC BLEU - LES HAUDÈRES - LA SAGE

Distance:	10 kilometres	
Time:	4 hours	
Start altitude:	1998m	*Low point:* Les Haudères 1452m
Height loss:	546m	*Height gain:* 215m
Maps:	L.S. 5003 Mont Blanc - Grand Combin and	
	5006 Matterhorn - Mischabel both 1:50,000	
Accommodation:	La Gouille (1 hour 45 mins) - pension	
	Les Haudères (3 hrs) - hotels, pension, dortoir,	
	camping	
	La Sage - hotel, dortoir	
	Villa (+ 15 mins) - simple rooms	
Transport options:	Postbus (Arolla -Les Haudères - La Sage)	

A gentle, undemanding stage, it is not really practical to go beyond La Sage (or Villa) on this walk as the crossing of Col de Torrent offers no accommodation possibilities in less than about 7 hours from La Sage. It is nonetheless a stage to wander slowly, to enjoy the 'holiday' aspect of the route and to give time to study the various features that brighten the way.

The walk to Les Haudères by way of Lac Bleu is designed to avoid the necessity of wandering along the tarmac road, and also in order to visit this little tarn which is one of the best-loved sites around Arolla. There are lovely views when you gaze back the way you have come. There are woodlands and small meadows, and between Lac Bleu and La Gouille a small alp hamlet where you can buy fresh milk and cheese. From La Gouille a wooded path leads to some splendid old houses on the edge of Les Haudères, a mountaineering centre at the head of Val d'Hérens where the valley forks into the tribuary glens of Arolla and Ferpècle. Then, leaving Les Haudères, a steady rising traverse path ascends the hillside to La Sage.

Note: *Before setting out on this stage it is advisable to telephone ahead to* *book rooms for the night. There is only limited accommodation in both La Sage and Villa. Failure to ensure beds in either of these places will necessitate returning to Les Haudéres, or going off-route to La Forclaz. In either eventuality, it might be worth taking the Postbus early next morning as far as Villa, there to begin the crossing of Col de Torrent.*

✳   ✳   ✳

From the main village square by the Post Office in Arolla walk down the side road towards Hotel du Glacier. About 50m before the hotel bear left on a narrow footpath which climbs above some buildings, then bears right along the hillside, soon to reach the Centre Alpin. Take the footpath ahead along the wooded hillside. Soon come to a junction of paths and bear right on an easy contour above the valley among larch and juniper. The path forks. Bear left and wind uphill on a comfortable gradient, soon crossing a stream below an alp hamlet. Beyond this the trail continues as a traverse of open hillside where it is worth pausing to enjoy the views back to Mont Collon and Pigne d'Arolla.

The route develops into something of a switchback, an undulating trail along the hillside that absorbs the natural line and takes you over two or three more streams, then onto an open grassy bluff overlooking the aptly-named **LAC BLEU** (2090, 1½ hours). Once again there's a fine view back to Mont Collon, although Pigne d'Arolla has disappeared at this point.

Alternative Route (Cabane des Aiguilles Rouges to Lac Bleu:)
Go above the hut on a rising path a short way heading north (direction arrows painted on rocks), then drop steeply, first towards the east to cross a stream, then south-eastwards on a clear path. Descending steeply through different layers of vegetation the way brings you directly to **LAC BLEU** (1 hour).

Go down to the eastern outflow end of the tarn and along the footpath to a tiny alp hamlet (**LOUCHE**) where cheese and milk

The classic view of Mont Collon from Pra Gra chalets on the descent from the Pas de Chèvres (Alternative Stage 7a)

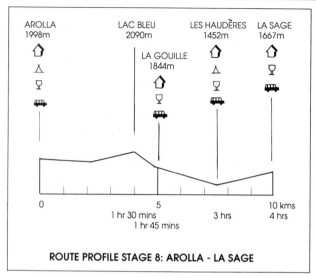

AROLLA 1998m
LAC BLEU 2090m
LES HAUDÈRES 1452m
LA SAGE 1667m
LA GOUILLE 1844m

0   5   10 kms
1 hr 30 mins   3 hrs   4 hrs
1 hr 45 mins

ROUTE PROFILE STAGE 8: AROLLA - LA SAGE

may be purchased. Pass to the right of the hamlet and descend through forest to **LA GOUILLE** (1844m 1 hour 45 mins *accommodation, refreshments, Postbus to Les Haudères*), a small village beside the Arolla/Les Haudères road. Bear left and walk down the road for about 200 metres, then slope off to the right on a path waymarked with yellow and black. This eases along the hillside below the road and soon reaches a clear track a few paces from a tiny white-painted chapel snug beneath an overhanging boulder. Continue down the track, and when it forks wander straight ahead.

With gentle gradients the track leads down-valley and eventually comes to a group of handsome old timber houses. Just beyond these join the main road, bear right and walk into **LES HAUDÈRES**.

(1) **LES HAUDÈRES** (1452m 3 hours) *Accommodation, camping, refreshments, shops, PTT, Postbus. Office du Tourisme, 1961 Les Haudères Tel: (027) 83 10 15). Lower priced hotels: des Alpes (027) 83 16 77; Garni Gai Logis (027) 83 14 13; Edelweiss (027) 83 11 07 - Dortoir at Colonie La Foret (027) 83 10 47*

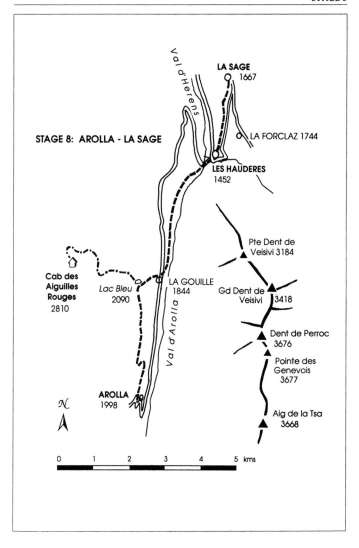

LA SAGE 1667

Val d'Herens

LA FORCLAZ 1744

STAGE 8: AROLLA - LA SAGE

LES HAUDERES 1452

Pte Dent de Veisivi 3184

Cab des
Aiguilles
Rouges
2810

Lac Bleu
2090

LA GOUILLE
1844

Gd Dent de
Veisivi 3418

Val d'Arolla

Dent de Perroc
3676

Pointe des
Genevois
3677

AROLLA
1998

𝒩

Aig de la Tsa
3668

0   1   2   3   4   5 kms

La Sage

On crossing the bridge at the entrance to the village bear right on the road heading towards Ferpècle, La Forclaz and La Sage, but soon turn off this to the left opposite Hotel des Alpes. Wander along a narrow street lined with attractive timber buildings, and follow through on an upper village street where there are both direction signs and waymarks.

It's an interesting stroll, for it takes you past some of the oldest and best of Les Haudères's buildings, then up above the village a track continues at the same steady angle, soon among trees. When it bends sharply to the right leave the track for a path continuing straight ahead. When this forks take the upper, right-hand path which will lead between meadows and onto the road near La Sage.

Almost immediately take a narrow tarmac road on the left. It winds through pastures and brings you to LA SAGE.

(2) **LA SAGE** (1667m 4 hours) *Accommodation, refreshments, shop, PTT, Postbus. Office du Tourisme, 1961 La Sage Tel: (027) 83 12 80. Hotel*

de La Sage (027) 83 11 10 (pre-arranged groups only) - dortoir at Les Ecureuils (027) 83 12 98

Note: Limited accommodation (self-catering) is available at the next village along the road (15 mins from La Sage), **VILLA**. Apply at the small shop as you enter the village, or contact: Fam. Maurice Gaudin, 1961 Villa/La Sage (027) 83 13 57.

✳ ✳ ✳

Places or Features of Interest Along the Way:

1. **LES HAUDÈRES**: This attractive, typical Valaisian village is mostly contained in a triangle delineated by two roads and a steep hillside at the head of Val d'Hérens. Most of its buildings are of timber on a stone base, with granaries mingled among the houses. The granaries stand on staddle stones to deter rodents. The village makes a good base for a walking holiday, the two adjacent valleys (of Arolla and Ferpècle) being of especial interest and with superb high mountain views.

2. **LA SAGE**: This small village is perched on a natural terrace some 250 metres above the valley. From it there are grand views across the head of the valley towards Pigne d'Arolla, or south-east to the snowfields and glaciers that spread between Dent Blanche and the ridge of the Bouquetins.

STAGE 9:
LA SAGE - COL de TORRENT - LAC de MOIRY - CABANE de MOIRY

Distance:	14 kilometres	
Time:	7-7½ hours	
Start altitude:	1667m	*High point:* Col de Torrent 2919m
Height gain:	1828m	*Height loss:* 670m
Accommodation:	Villa (15 mins) - self-catering rooms	
	Cabane de Moiry - SAC refuge	
Map	L.S. 5006 Matterhorn - Mischabel 1:50,000	
Transport options:	None	

Between Val d'Hérens and Val d'Anniviers, the next major valley on the journey heading east, there sidles the small but lovely Val de Moiry - a tributary glen that feeds Anniviers. To walk from one to the other entails a crossing of the long ridge system that extends north-westward from the Grand Cornier, a mountain whose other northerly ridge also effectively divides the Moiry glen from that of Val d'Anniviers. The north-west ridge, although maintaining an altitude of 2900 metres and more as far north as Sasseneire, nonetheless contains several crossing points, Col de Torrent (2919m) being the most accessible.

A long and somewhat arduous stage, this is however, one of the most visually spectacular of them all. Magnificent views accompany you to the col, while on the eastern side a grand panorama, equal to almost anything seen so far, draws you to it. On the Val d'Hérens flank the whole ascent is over steep slopes of pasture - a living, working landscape. Val de Moiry, on the other hand, is wild and glacial at its head, yet to get there entails a descent through more gentle pastures tended by local farmers.

Approach to the Moiry hut is somewhat wearying at the end of a longish day, but it is perched in such a spectacular position that all effort to reach it will be considered well-worthwhile. From the hut the walker gains an

Villa with the Dent Blanche in the background

amazing head-on view of the Moiry icefall and experiences the arctic world of the high mountains normally reserved only for full-blooded mountaineers. Of all lodgings on the Chamonix-Zermatt walk, Cabane de Moiry must rank among the finest for its setting.

Note: *Beyond Villa there are no opportunities for refreshment, so a full water bottle should be taken - as should spare films for the camera.*

*   *   *

Walk up the road from La Sage to **VILLA**. (1714m 15 mins *accommodation, refreshments, shops, Postbus. Note: the food store next to the restaurant at the northern end of the village is open all day on Sundays.*)

Just across the bridge in Villa you come to a small white chapel on the left of the road. Turn immediately opposite this to walk between two granaries on the right, and then head uphill on a cobbled track. The cobbles finish at the upper end of the village, but a track continues. A footpath then leads on from this, climbing the steeply sloping hillside.

From the very start views are grand; not just to those peaks

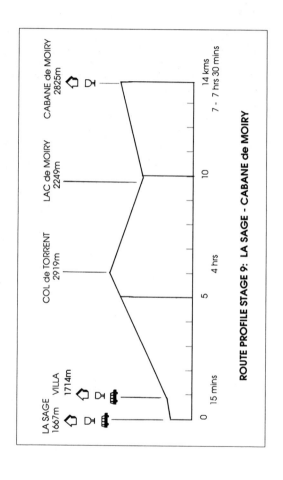

ROUTE PROFILE STAGE 9: LA SAGE - CABANE de MOIRY

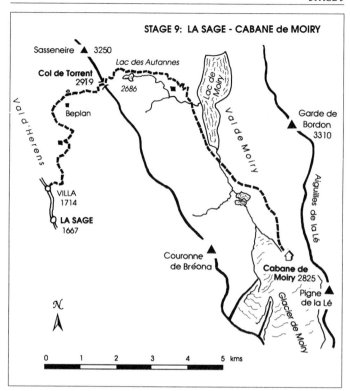

STAGE 9: LA SAGE - CABANE de MOIRY

Sasseneire ▲ 3250

Lac des Autannes

Col de Torrent
2919

2686

Beplan

Val d'Hérens

Lac de Moiry

Val de Moiry

Garde de
Bordon
▲ 3310

Aiguilles de la Lé

VILLA
1714

LA SAGE
1667

Couronne
de Bréona ▲

⬦
Cabane de
Moiry 2825

Pigne
de la Lé ▲

Glacier de Moiry

𝒩

0   1   2   3   4   5 kms

behind that have become familiar from walking beside them during
the past few days, but ahead too, to mountains of the Bernese Alps
on the far side of the Rhône valley. Les Diablerets and the Wildhorn
massif look especially fine.

The path brings you to a track beyond a small chalet. Turn right
here, but round the next bend where the track forks, take the left-
hand branch. This winds between pastures and leads to an alp
hamlet and yet another track (2160m). Bear left, and in a few paces
take a rising path on the right above a water trough.

Gaining height, sometimes steeply, you pass below a small

105

isolated hut near some pillars of upstanding rock. This is **BEPLAN** (2486m 1 hours 45 mins). The trail winds round to the right where you enter a high alp pasture with another hut seen off to the left. Continuing you soon reach a small pond (2536m), and from it Col de Torrent is seen as a modest saddle above to the right. Wandering up in long loops, steeply now and then, you continue over high pastures and then at last come onto **COL de TORRENT** (2919m 3-4 hours).

Warm from our morning's exertions and the bright sunshine we dumped the rucksacks at the col and gave ourselves to the views and the day. It was, yet again, a day of unbelievable clarity; of blue skies and sunshine, the sort of day you dream about at home when planning a walk such as this, but which is too seldom translated into reality. Yet on the Col de Torrent we had all we could wish. Those views, for example. To south and west the panorama included the Tête Blanche, Grande Dent de Veisivi, Mont Brulé, Pigne d'Arolla, Mont Blanc de Cheilon, Grand Combin, the Aiguilles Rouges, Rosablanche and the Grand Désert glacier, while far off we could make out the snowy mass of Mont Blanc itself. Turning to the east we recognised the Weisshorn, of fond memory; the Schalihorn and Blanc de Moming. But lying between us and them was the deep trough of Val de Moiry and the next ridge beyond it. Below shone the Lac des Autannes from its pastureland bed; beyond that the jade waters of the dammed Lac de Moiry. Tomorrow we would be in the shadow of the Weisshorn. Today we had all the magic of the Moiry glen before us, and with prospects of making a return visit to the hut so majestically set among the glaciers near its head, we looked to the descent with a smile on our faces.

Note: For an even broader panorama than that won from the col, go left up the ridge for 45 minutes to the summit of Sasseneire (3250m). But only if you have the energy and time to spare. You'll need about $1^{1}/_{2}$ hours for the round trip.

A clear path descends on the Moiry side, first heading north, then swinging eastward down to undulating pastureland. As you draw level with the picturesque Lac des Autannes, some 230 metres or so below the col, exquisite views are to be had across its dazzling waters to a turmoil of glaciers and a clutch of shapely peaks that block the head of [1] Val de Moiry. Up there, Pigne de la Lé and Grand Cornier throw out ridges, snowfields and long streamers of ice, creating those contrasts of light and shade, height and depth, barren upland against a foreground of soft pasture, that make wandering in the Alps such a memorable feast of beauty.

On coming to a farm (**MONTAGNE de TORRENT** 2481m) a choice of routes is offered. Either follow a sign-posted path in front of the farm building - this takes you above the Lac de Moiry at about 2500m, and in one place is protected with chains, descends (yellow waymarks) to a junction of trails where you take the left-hand path down to the lakes at the foot of the glacier. The way to the hut is obvious from here. Alternatively, join a track and wander down it for about 400 metres, then turn abruptly from it onto a dirt farm track that breaks away to the right. (The continuing main track is that which is followed on Alternative Stage 9 to Grimentz.) You are now led back into a pastureland basin, and as you enter it, leave the track and go left to cross a stream and join a clear path sloping down towards Lac de Moiry. On coming to a lakeside path bear right, and at the end of the lake continue to a metal bridge which takes you over a charming glacial stream. ($1\frac{1}{2}$ hours from Col de Torrent. Cabane de Moiry is 1 hour 45 mins from here.)

Having crossed the footbridge bear right to follow a track, then a footpath which leads up onto a road. Cross the road onto a continuing path. This winds up and over rough boulder-pocked grassland and eventually comes to the lateral moraine bordering the eastern side of Glacier de Moiry. The trail goes along the very crest of the moraine, descends the left-hand slope and then begins a tiring zig-zag climb to the hut. The path is clear and waymarked right to the boulder-strewn shelf on which sits **CABANE de MOIRY** facing the magnificent icefall of the [2] Moiry glacier.

[3] **CABANE de MOIRY** (2825m 7-7$\frac{1}{2}$ hours) *100 places, meals and drinks when the guardian is in residence, from the end of June to end of September. Tel: (027) 83 10 18*

* * *

The Cabane de Moiry

Places or Features of Interest Along the Way:

1. **VAL de MOIRY:** This small glen feeds the long Val d'Anniviers, of which it forms the south-western tributary. It rises in a tight wedge of peaks whose nodal point is the Grand Cornier (3962m), and in whose upper ridges a basin of névé gives birth to the Moiry glacier. Below the glacier two small tarns are used as settlement reservoirs to reduce the flow of glacial silt into the larger dammed Lac de Moiry below. A road follows the eastern side of the lake from the barrage, and goes as far as the smaller tarns where the cars of climbers are often parked. Below the barrage the glen is somewhat wild, but it grows green and wooded towards Grimentz, an attractive village near the mouth of the valley. Grimentz is the only village in the Val de Moiry.

2. **MOIRY ICEFALL:** The icefall of the Moiry glacier is among the most impressive of its kind in the Pennine Alps, and that the mountain walker can gaze upon it from so close and safe a vantage point as the hut, makes it extra special. In *The Alps in 1864*, that great

Victorian pioneer A W Moore wrote about this in glowing terms, referring to it as: "...a tremendous ice-fall of great height and very steep. The lower part... extends completely from one side of the glacier to the other, but higher up, under the Pigne de la Lex, is a belt of smooth ice, which we had no doubt would give access to the field of névé above the fall. Below this great cascade of séracs, the ice is as compact and level as above it is steep and dislocated. Indeed, I never saw an ice-fall confined within such plainly defined limits, or terminate so abruptly."

3. **CABANE de MOIRY:** Owned by the Montreux section of the Swiss Alpine Club, the Moiry hut enjoys a most dramatic situation among a horseshoe of peaks and glaciers. Above it to the east runs the wall of the Aiguilles de la Lé; opposite rise Couronne de Bréona, Pointe de Moiry and Tsa de l'Ano. Between the Couronne and Pointe de Moiry lies the Col de la Couronne by which access to the glen may be achieved from the head of Val d'Hérens (a more strenuous and less well-marked route than that over Col de Torrent), while south-east of the hut, between the last of the Aiguilles de la Lé and Pigne de la Lé, Col du Pigne offers another way over to Zinal. (Not for inexperienced mountain walkers though.) The hut is popular among ski-mountaineers, for several of the summits that enclose the glacier provide enjoyable ski tours. Pigne de la Lé and Pointe de Bricola (north-west of Grand Cornier) are among the most popular, while summer ascents are made directly from the hut to Grand Cornier and all the neighbouring peaks. By virtue of its short approach from the roadhead ($1^{1}/_{2}$ hours), Cabane de Moiry has plenty of day-visitors.

ALTERNATIVE STAGE 9:
LA SAGE - COL de TORRENT - BARRAGE de MOIRY - GRIMENTZ

Distance:	14 kilometres	
Time:	6^1/$_2$-7 hours	
Start altitude:	1667m	*High point:* Col de Torrent 2919m
Height gain:	1252m	*Height loss:* 1347m
Map:	L.S. 5006 Matterhorn - Mischabel 1:50,000	
Accommodation:	Villa (15 mins) - self-catering rooms	
	Barrage de Moiry (5 hours) - dortoir	
	Grimentz - hotels, dortoir	
Transport options:	Postbus (Barrage de Moiry-Grimentz)	

Several organised parties of walkers choose to avoid the crossing of Col de Sorebois between Val de Moiry and Val de Zinal on Stage 10, by heading north to skirt the projecting ridge that divides Moiry from Anniviers. In my opinion this is a grave error of judgement - other than in severe weather conditions - for the views from the col are quite outstanding, even by the high standards set elsewhere along this walk. But this circuitous alternative via Grimentz does at least give the opportunity to admire an extremely attractive village and provides one or two options for the continuing route.

By choosing this route, the question then arises with regard to the next day's stage, for you are faced with either a road walk to Mission (from where the ascent to Hotel Weisshorn can be made), a woodland walk to Zinal, or a bus ride round to Val d'Anniviers. None of these options remains true to the spirit of an Haute Route to Zermatt, but walkers must make their own choice. This alternative is offered in the event of bad weather effectively making Col de Sorebois a non-viable option.

* * *

Follow directions as given for Stage 9 over Col de Torrent and down to the track leading below the farm, **MONTAGNE de TORRENT**

(2481m). Instead of breaking away from this track, continue with it all the way to the dam at the northern end of Lac de Moiry. At this **BARRAGE de MOIRY** (2249m 5 hours *accommodation - dortoir for groups in Chalet du Barrage (027) 65 15 48 - refreshments, w.c., public telephone, Postbus to Grimentz*) descend the clear path below the dam wall to join the road, which you follow for a little over 2 kilometres. Leave the road (at **MOIRETTE** 1973m) to wander down a path on the right. This takes you into the bed of the valley, across the stream and continues on the right bank until shortly before reaching **GRIMENTZ**, when a bridge returns you to the left bank and up to the road again on the outskirts of the village.

[1] **GRIMENTZ** (1572m 6½-7 hours) *Accommodation, refreshments, shops, bank, PTT, Postbus (to Zinal, St Luc, Vissoie, Sierre). Office du Tourisme, 3961 Grimentz Tel: (027) 65 14 93. Dortoirs for groups: Chalet Bleu (027) 65 23 23; Chalet Bouquetin (027) 65 15 27. Lower priced hotels: Bouquetin (027) 65 15 27; Marenda (027) 65 11 71; Mélèze (027) 65 12 87 Note:* A waymarked route leads from Grimentz to Zinal (8 kms) in 2½ hours.

* * *

Places or Features of Interest Along the Way:
1. **GRIMENTZ:** Reckoned to be one of the most attractive villages in the canton of Valais, its narrow alleys edge between dark timber houses from whose windows bright boxes of geraniums and petunias seem to light every building. The village is growing in an effort to entice more winter visitors and it remains to be seen how such developments will affect the tranquillity of the place. There are cableways (gondola and chair-lift) leading to a hillside laced with drag lifts for winter use. But the village also has a heated indoor swimming pool that may be utilized by the summer walker choosing Grimentz for an overnight rest.

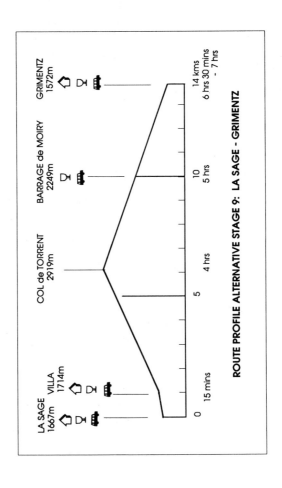

ROUTE PROFILE ALTERNATIVE STAGE 9: LA SAGE - GRIMENTZ

The vast panorama of the Pennine Alps seen from the Pas de Chèvres. On the left is the Dent Blanche with the needle-like Aiguille de la Tsa in front of it. On the right is the Matterhorn with the Dent d'Hérens to the right again and the jagged Bouquetins in front. Arolla lies in the valley below (Alt. Stage 7a).
(Walt Unsworth)

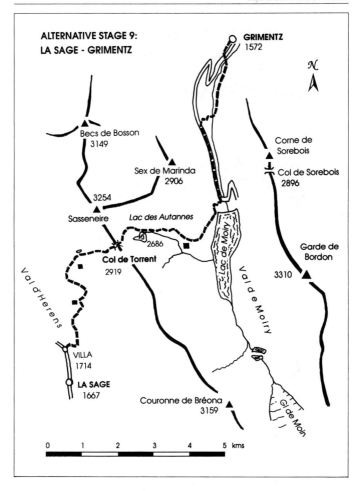

**ALTERNATIVE STAGE 9:
LA SAGE - GRIMENTZ**

GRIMENTZ
1572

N

Becs de Bosson
3149

Sex de Marinda
2906

Corne de
Sorebois

Col de Sorebois
2896

3254

Sasseneire   *Lac des Autannes*

2686

Garde de
Bordon

Col de Torrent
2919

3310

Val d'Herens

Val de Moiry

Lac de Moiry

VILLA
1714

LA SAGE
1667

Couronne de Bréona
3159

Gl de Moin

0   1   2   3   4   5 kms

*The classic view of Mont Collon from Pra Gra chalets on the descent
from the Pas de Chèvres (Alternative Stage 7a)*

113

STAGE 10:
CABANE de MOIRY - COL de SOREBOIS - ZINAL

Distance:	13 kilometres	
Time:	5¹/₂-6 hours	
Start altitude:	2825m	*High point:* Col de Sorebois 2896m
Height gain:	647m	*Height loss:* 1797m
Map:	L.S. 5006 Matterhorn - Mischabel 1:50,000	
Accommodation:	Barrage de Moiry (2 hours) - dortoir for groups	
	Cabane de Sorebois (4¹/₂ hours) - dortoir	
	Zinal - hotels, pensions, dortoir, camping	
Transport options:	Postbus (Barrage de Moiry-Grimentz-Zinal)	
	Cable-car (Sorebois-Zinal)	

From the arctic splendour of the upper Val de Moiry to the deep forested trench of Val de Zinal (the upper reaches of Val d'Anniviers) entails the crossing of yet another high ridge. This, however, is rather less demanding than the approach to Col de Torrent on Stage 9, but the vista that greets you on arrival at Col de Sorebois is every bit as spectacular as that from yesterday's pass. By now there are few superlatives left with which to describe the wonder of this mountain scenery. Surely no walker could fail to be moved by the sight of the Weisshorn and Zinalrothorn hovering across the valley? And it is only the efforts of man to turn the hillside below into a winter playground that adds a sober punctuation to an otherwise glorious belvedere.

Walking from Cabane de Moiry to Col de Sorebois formerly meant a return down-valley as far as the barrage at the northern end of the lake - thereby losing more than 500 metres of height; height that immediately had to be regained. There is now an alternative trail that avoids this. The climb to the pass is not unduly fatiguing, while the descent to Zinal seems only to become steeper as you lose height. As you descend, though, all physical effort is subdued by the beauty of the mountains opposite and the expanding

Descending into Zinal from the Col de Sorebois

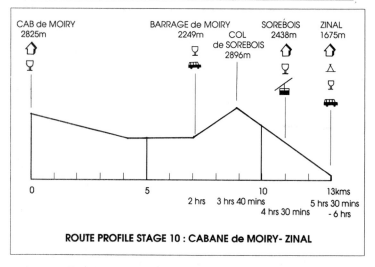

ROUTE PROFILE STAGE 10 : CABANE de MOIRY- ZINAL

view upvalley which gives a foretaste of tomorrow's scenic pleasures.

It's a comparatively easy walk, and at the same time is one of those rare stages when it is possible to buy refreshment along the way; first at a restaurant at the dam, then about an hour above Zinal at the Sorebois cable-car station.

There are two ways of gaining Col de Sorebois from the hut. The first is more direct and avoids a tedious stretch of road-walking. The second is the traditional route.

Route a: Descend from the hut until you come to a signposted junction of trails. The Col de Sorebois/Zinal path follows a regular contour at about 2500 metres, keeping well above the lake, and eventually joins the alternative route between the dam and the pass.

Route b: Descend from the hut on the same route used for the approach, taking care if there has been frost overnight as the upper rocks that form the path may well be glazed. Upon reaching Lac de Moiry wander along the road that skirts its eastern shore. A few

116

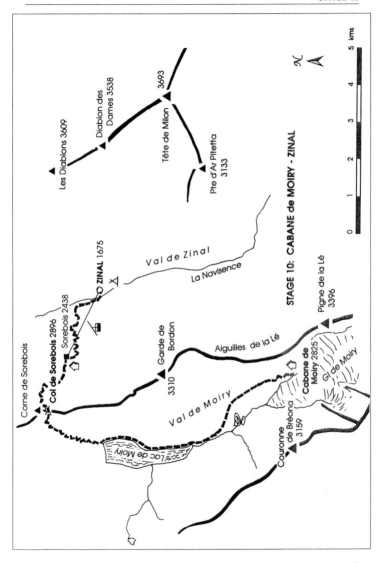

Les Diablons 3609

Diablon des Dames 3538

3693

Tête de Milon

Pte d'Ar Pitetta 3133

ZINAL 1675

Val de Zinal

La Navisence

STAGE 10: CABANE de MOIRY - ZINAL

Corne de Sorebois

Sorebois 2438

Col de Sorebois 2896

Garde de Bordon 3310

Aiguilles de la Lé

Pigne de la Lé 3396

Val de Moiry

Lac de Moiry

Cabane de Moiry 2825

Gl de Moiry

Couronne de Bréona 3159

0 1 2 3 4 5 kms

N

metres from the **BARRAGE de MOIRY** (2249m 2 hours *dortoir accommodation for groups - Chalet du Barrage (027) 65 15 48 - refreshments, w.c., public telephone, Postbus to Zinal via St-Jean and Vissoie*) leave the road for a track rising ahead above the dam car park.

Walk up the track, then break away onto a second track on the right when a painted sign on a rock indicates the route to Sorebois. A footpath leads off from this, going ahead. The way now continues as a combination of footpath and track with very few waymarks. It is important to avoid following either of two tracks that lead far off to the right (south), but instead maintain a steady course going roughly north-east. There is a faint path that grows more evident as you gain height. At times this trail is quite steep with zig-zags, but is pleasant all the way. Views are mostly down-valley towards Grimentz. There is a good possibility of catching sight of chamois and marmots here.

Come onto the saddle of **COL de SOREBOIS** (2896m 3 hours 40 mins) where you will find a signpost. But of more interest than times and destinations shown on this is the astonishing panorama of high peaks opposite, dominated by the [1] Weisshorn. Ignore the ski grounds below and, like the Psalmist, lift your eyes to the hills, for this is one of the finest views so far. (A phrase that seems to have been repeated once or twice already; but such is the nature of this walk that the scenery begins on a high note and gets even better!) The collection of peaks in view back towards the south-west includes many that have grown familiar over the preceding days, and it is amusing to put a name to them all.

To descend into [2] Val de Zinal, first bear left and rise a short way along the ridge, then slant right on a track (a broad ski piste) that begins the descent route proper to Zinal village and goes in long windings down to the Sorebois cableway station.

It must be said that the piste makes for easy walking, but it is a shameful example of the sacrifices forced on the mountain environment on behalf of the ski industry. Yet lessons have at last been learnt and as you wander down it is worth considering what has happened here. For years these slopes were grubbed bare, first by bulldozers, then by constant use by skiers over several winter months. Erosion was more than an eyesore once the snow had melted. However, these pistes have now been seeded and the effects of this remedial action are already evident, for on Stage 11 as you wander the far side of the valley, the scars of erosion are barely visible, while not so long ago they appeared like roadways on the hillside. So, whilst one may well deplore the existence of bulldozed pistes in the first place, it is encouraging to acknowledge there is activity to redress the balance. Elsewhere in the valley similar work is going on to make good man's mistakes. There is, then, some room for optimism. (If only the skeleton hoists that march so blatantly up the hillside were removed each spring!)

On coming to **SOREBOIS** (2438m 4½ hours dortoir accommodation - (027) 65 13 78 - refreshments, cable-car to Zinal) bear right and find the signposted track/path that winds down in zig-zags to and fro beneath the cableway, then enters forest where the way becomes even steeper - something of a knee-jarring descent. The path is clear and obvious and it brings you to a footbridge over the Navisence stream and up into **ZINAL**.

(3) **ZINAL** (1675m 5½-6 hours) *Accommodation, camping, refreshments, shops, bank, PTT, Postbus (Zinal-Vissoie-St Luc-Sierre). Office du Tourisme, 3961 Zinal (027) 65 13 70. Dortoir at Auberge Alpina (027) 65 12 24; Lower-priced hotels: Auberge Alpina; Hotel de la Poste (027) 65 11 87; Hotel Les Bouquetins (027) 65 25 09. Also in Pralong (2 kms north), Pension de Pralong (027) 65 11 86*

*   *   *

Places or Features of Interest Along the Way:

1. **WEISSHORN:** A beautiful mountain bearing three faces and three ridges, at 4505 metres it ranks as one of the highest in the Pennine Alps. Standing on that great ridge which separates Val de Zinal from that of the Mattertal, the Weisshorn is eye-catching from several different angles, and will be seen to great dramatic effect later, on the penultimate stage of the walk. As a mountaineer's mountain the main interest lies in its ridges, for the faces hold little of technical interest. It was first climbed by the pioneering Victorian scientist and mountaineer John Tyndall (1820-93) in 1861, with J J Bennen and U Wenger as his guides.

2. **VAL DE ZINAL:** The name given to the upper reaches of Val d'Anniviers, Val de Zinal holds much of interest to both walkers and climbers. Indeed, some of the most varied and scenically spectacular walks in the whole Pennine Alps are to be enjoyed here, while the big peaks that wall it hold some dramatic routes. The head of the valley is a spectacular amphitheatre of ice and snow with Ober Gabelhorn, Mont Durand, Pointe de Zinal, Dent Blanche, Grand Cornier and the Bouquetins rising from it. Zinalrothorn, Pointe Sud de Moming, Schalihorn and Weisshorn create another cirque in the south-east, while opposite this is the pasture bowl of La Lé with a rocky crescent above that. Evidence of the work of past glaciations is clearly to be read in the valley itself.

3. **ZINAL:** A growing village and long-time mountaineering centre, it spreads along the right bank of the valley with a succession of timber houses and barns showing their age, while a more recent development has sprung up at the northern end. Zinal makes a first-rate base for a walking or climbing holiday.

STAGE 11:
ZINAL - HOTEL WEISSHORN

Distance:	10 kilometres	
Time:	4 hours	
Start altitude:	1675m	*High point:* Montagne de Nava 2400m
Height gain:	725m	*Height loss:* 63m
Map:	L.S. 5006 Matterhorn - Mischabel 1:50,000	
Accommodation:	Hotel Weisshorn	
Transport options:	Postbus (Zinal-Vissoie-St Luc)	
	Chair-lift (St Luc-Tignousa)	

*If you are running short of days (limited perhaps by bad weather), it would
be feasible to combine this comparatively easy walk with Stage 12 as far as
the Turtmanntal or, better than that, follow Alternative Stage 11 direct to
Gruben-Meiden. It would be a great shame to do so, however, for the route
is such a magical one that its pleasures ought to be absorbed slowly. It
would also be a pity to miss the experience of a night spent in the eccentric
Victorian building of Hotel Weisshorn, which has become something of an
institution among mountain wanderers.*

*The path runs along a shelf of hillside way above the Val d'Anniviers
and presents such stunning views to the head of the valley that you begin
to wish it were possible to walk backwards or, failing that, have a wing
mirror in order not to miss the splendour of the high mountain scenery.*

*By virtue of the scenery in the south this particular section ought really
to be walked the other way round, in reverse, so to speak. With a route going
from Chamonix to Zermatt, that becomes impractical, of course. But that
is yet another reason for taking it slowly; wander the path staccato fashion,
stopping frequently to capture the magic of the deep Val d'Anniviers rising
to the great mass of snow and ice giants at its head, for this is a view that
must rank among the finest to be experienced anywhere; it is certainly one
of the most exciting visions I know. (In writing these words I am fully*

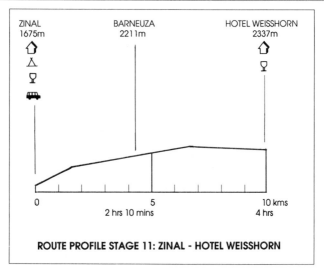

ROUTE PROFILE STAGE 11: ZINAL - HOTEL WEISSHORN

aware that there will be some walkers reading this preamble on a damp, grey morning in Zinal with no prospects whatsoever of seeing those views on their way to Hotel Weisshorn. I can only commiserate and sincerely hope that you will gain pleasures on the way even without the benefit of blue skies and sunshine, and at the same time urge you to return to the valley on some future holiday. Not only to allow the weather to make amends, so far as this particular route is concerned, but also to explore further. Zinal has more than its fair share of stunningly beautiful day walks.)

From the centre of Zinal, near Hotel Le Besso, walk up a narrow side street to pass beside the church, and 100 metres beyond this bear left on a track near a large hotel/apartment block. (This area is being developed at the time of writing, so changes may occur here to alter the route slightly.) The track brings you to another narrow road by a modern hotel/chalet complex named *Formule 1*. Cross the road and walk straight ahead up a narrow road/driveway signposted to Hotel Weisshorn. Above the buildings take a waymarked track

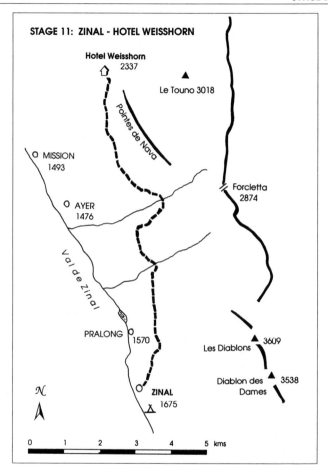

STAGE 11: ZINAL - HOTEL WEISSHORN

Hotel Weisshorn
2337

Le Touno 3018

Pointes de Nava

MISSION
1493

Forcletta
2874

AYER
1476

Val de Zinal

PRALONG 1570

Les Diablons 3609

Diablon des 3538
Dames

ZINAL
1675

𝒩

0 1 2 3 4 5 kms

heading to the right and rising among stands of larch, soon to cross an avalanche defence system.

Once across this the path, broad and well-trodden, begins to make height in forest shade. With a series of steep zig-zags you soon rise high above the valley, and about 50 minutes from Zinal the route takes pity and eases itself into a more gentle rising traverse. In 1 hour 15 minutes from the start you come out of the trees and onto a lovely open shelf of hillside (2173m) with a charming view back to Pigne de la Lé, Grand Cornier and Dent Blanche, while ahead you gaze across the Rhône valley to the line of the Bernese Alps.

The path now develops as a superb belvedere heading north along the hillside, and in due course you will reach a lonely little farm (**BARNEUZA ALPAGE** 2211m 2 hours 10 mins). Immediately beyond the alp buildings the path forks. Now continue ahead on the upper, right-hand trail. This eventually cuts deeply into a combe of hillside, crosses a stream and comes to the hut of **ALPE NAVA** (2340m 2 hours 40 mins). Again the path forks, but this time the alternative route heads up to cross the Pas de Forcletta, by which Gruben in the Turtmanntal (Alternative Stage 11) may be reached in 4$^{1}/_{2}$ hours. But this option is ignored and the continuing path to Hotel Weisshorn goes straight ahead.

On this next section the panorama of peaks to the south grows even more impressive and includes the Zinalrothorn, Ober Gabelhorn, Matterhorn, Dent Blanche etc. It is worth many halts to enjoy this view, rather than keep your back to it and plough on regardless.

We were on course for setting a record for the slowest-ever walk from Zinal to Hotel Weisshorn. Our day was rather like Morse code, a succession of dots and dashes as we stumbled along the path among autumn-tinged bilberry leaves shining with a burst of scarlet, then collapsed in a delirium as the mountain panorama behind us demanded another token of appreciation. Progress was painfully slow that day, but who cared? Not I, for one. For no matter how many mountain ranges I'd visited in the past, no matter how many views had won my heart, what was spread before me - before us - was a priceless gem of perfection, an unsurpassed, unparalleled vision of glory. Our horizon was an upthrust of spires and domes, a patchwork of grey rock and pure snow, of gleaming ice and deep blue shadow drawn into wonder by a September sky dusted and scrubbed clean. Down below the valley had been hushed with early frost, then it had sparkled as the frost turned to moisture. Now it was dry in the sunlight;

The Zinal valley seen from the path to the Hotel Weisshorn

dark swathes of forest lapped against the lower slopes. Bare grass textured the upper levels opposite with velvet. Then rock. And snow and ice far off. Way up there at the head of the valley was the birthplace of glaciers, and all down the Val d'Anniviers we could see a tribute to their industry. It was all far too good to ignore. There could be no haste this day, for every step to the north was a pace away from that taste of heaven. Sacrilege, no less.

Rising still, but easily, you join a track and then continue ahead on a footpath running parallel to it, but at a higher level. (The track winds down to Ayer; the footpath is waymarked St Luc.) On coming to a second track by some avalanche defences, bear left along it, and shortly after take the path rising ahead. (By now you'll have lost the best views back to the head of the valley, although partial views will be restored later.)

The trail rises and falls over an undulating hillside and soon brings you in sight of Hotel Weisshorn, while an interesting inner mountain basin is seen off to the right. Just above the hotel join a track and bear left down it to come to **HOTEL WEISSHORN**.

[1] **HOTEL WEISSHORN** (2337m 4 hours) *50 beds , restaurant service. Open late June to end September. Reservations recommended in high season. Contact:*
Hotel Weisshorn, 3961 St Luc Tel: (027) 65 11 06

Note: In case of difficulty in finding accommodation here, Cabane de Bella Tola (120 places Tel: (027) 65 15 37) and Cabane Tignousa (24 dortoir places Tel: (027) 65 13 60) are both found to the north of Hotel Weisshorn, less than an hour's walk away.

* * *

Places or Features of Interest Along the Way:

1. **HOTEL WEISSHORN:** As mentioned in the introduction to this stage, Hotel Weisshorn is almost an institution. A large, imposing building dating from the 1880s, in a magnificent position more than a thousand metres above the valley bed. The Rhône valley lies to the north, and the southern wall of the Bernese Alps rises above that. Sunset views are particularly fine.

ALTERNATIVE STAGE 11:
ZINAL - FORCLETTA - GRUBEN-MEIDEN

Distance:	14 kilometres
Time:	6½-7 hours
Start altitude:	1675m *High point:* Forcletta 2874m
Height gain:	1199m *Height loss:* 1052m
Map:	L.S. 5006 Matterhorn - Mischabel 1:50,000
Accommodation:	Gruben-Meiden - hotel (beds & dortoirs) and dortoir
Transport options:	None

This option misses the chance to stay overnight in Hotel Weisshorn, but provides a most enjoyable and convenient crossing of the ridge separating Val de Zinal from the Turtmanntal. Any high route walkers needing to make up a lost day should consider tackling this stage. The way to the pass is not difficult, while the descent leads to some stunning views. All in all an enjoyable day's walking.

*   *   *

Follow Stage 11 as far as Alpe Nava (2 hours 40mins). Leave the main path here and take that which heads up to the right over grass slopes drained by a stream. The path (faint in places) skirts the right-hand slopes of a pastureland bowl and enters an upper level. Bear left, then rise to an alp farm (**TSAHALET** 2523m) with a large wooden cross above it. Behind the right-hand end of the cattle sheds red-white waymarks lead the continuing path across a rucked and pitted grassland. On the far side a clear path, now waymarked also with yellow diamonds outlined in black, leads up rocky slopes. The way climbs easily in long zig-zags to reach the **FORCLETTA** (2874m 4 hours 30 mins), a bare saddle in a ridge stubbed with rocky peaklets. Views east look down the length of the Blüomatttalli to the Turtmanntal running at right angles to it.

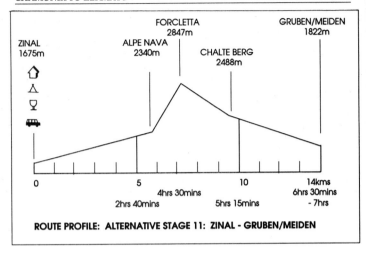

ROUTE PROFILE: ALTERNATIVE STAGE 11: ZINAL - GRUBEN/MEIDEN

Slant left from the pass across a slope of shale, then ease down the left-hand side of the shallow glen of Blüomatttalli. Towards the lower end of this glen the Brunegghorn comes into view to the right across the Turtmanntal, then its long glacier with the Bishorn looking huge to the right of that, and at last the Weisshorn rising above the Bishorn.

The way now veers left over rolling pastures and comes to the farm buildings of **CHALTE BERG** (2488m 5 hours 15 mins). Views of the Bishorn, Weisshorn and snow crest leading to the Tête de Milon are tremendous from here. Pass between the alp buildings where the way is guided by waymarks directly down the slope to an unmade farm road. Turn left, and in about 150 metres bear right on a footpath which descends a little, then runs parallel to the road, later dropping well below it to more alp huts (**MASSSTAFEL** 2235m). Come onto the road once more, walk down it a short distance, then break away to the right opposite the last hut. Cross the road again, then continue on a delightful descent through forest, finally coming to the valley bed by more farm buildings about a kilometre upvalley from Gruben. Cross the stream and walk down the road to **GRUBEN-MEIDEN**.

The Pigne d'Arolla seen from the path to the Col de Torrent (Stage 9)

The path out of Zinal to the Hotel Weisshorn reveals a superb mountain panorama. On the right is the Gd. Cornier and Dent Blanche. The Matterhorn is in the centre with the Dent d'Hérens on its right. The rocky Lo Besso is on the left, with the Zinal Rothorn and Obergabelhorn behind. (Stage 11).

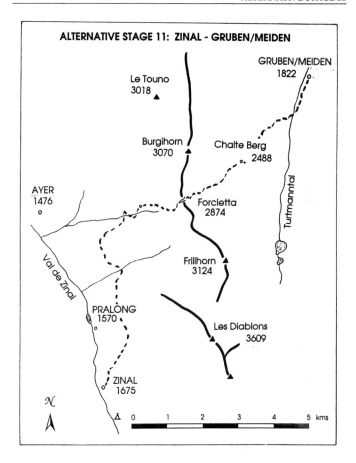

ALTERNATIVE STAGE 11: ZINAL - GRUBEN/MEIDEN

GRUBEN/MEIDEN
1822

Le Touno
3018

Burgihorn
3070

Chalte Berg
2488

AYER
1476

Forcletta
2874

Turtmanntal

Frilihorn
3124

Val de Zinal

PRALONG
1570

Les Diablons
3609

ZINAL
1675

N

0 1 2 3 4 5 kms

GRUBEN-MEIDEN (1822m 6½-7 hours) *Accommodation, refreshments, shop. Accommodation at Hotel Schwarzhorn (beds & matratzenlager/dortoirs) (028) 42 14 14 - Open June to October. Matratzenlager/dortoir also at Restaurant Waldesruh (5 minutes down valley from the village) (028) 42 13 27.*

Evening in Zermatt (Photo: Walt Unsworth)

STAGE 12:
HOTEL WEISSHORN - MEIDPASS - GRUBEN-MEIDEN

Distance:	9 kilometres		
Time:	4 hours		
Start altitude:	2337m	*High point:*	Meidpass 2790m
Height gain:	589m	*Height loss:*	1104m
Map:	L.S. 5006 Matterhorn - Mischabel 1:50,000		
Accommodation:	Gruben-Meiden - hotel (beds & dortoir)		
Transport options:	None		

This undemanding day's walk leads out of French-speaking Valais and into German-speaking Wallis; the same canton but linguistically a world apart from that through which you've been walking since crossing the Col de Balme.

And it's not just the language that changes either, for a different set of landscapes are in view - quite unlike anything yet seen on the walk. On leaving Hotel Weisshorn the way leads through a curiously contorted country en route to the Meidpass (or Meiden Pass as it is also known), while the way down to the Turtmanntal is a descent into the past. The Turtmanntal is, indeed, a remnant of a forgotten world, for within it you seem to have stepped back a hundred years. There is a road into the valley, it is true, and the hotel there has all modern amenities. Yet a profound sense of peace prevails and the whole valley seems to be quite undisturbed by the pressures of the modern world 'outside'. It is a valley easy to love.

*   *   *

Above Hotel Weisshorn follow the track as it curves round to the right, in effect retracing the very last stage of yesterday's approach. This delivers you to a view overlooking a geologically interesting basin opposite the 'island' peak of Le Touno (3018m). Continue beyond the initial signpost to a second where the route to Meidpass is first given. Wander down a track that winds leftwards through a

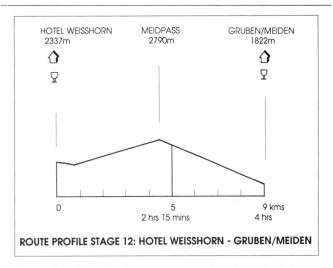

ROUTE PROFILE STAGE 12: HOTEL WEISSHORN - GRUBEN/MEIDEN

confused, chaotic patch of country scoured out by a glacial system whose icy remnants disappeared long ago. The track takes you below Le Touno, crosses a stream, then strikes northward until, about 30 minutes from Hotel Weisshorn, you come to a collection of old white stone alp buildings and a junction of tracks.

Go past the farm buildings for a few paces, then bear right on a vague signposted path towards the Meiden Pass, crossing a rough pastureland. As you gain height so the way becomes more distinct on a partial track. This leads to an isolated alp hut about 10 minutes above the previous alp buildings. The hut stands in a walled enclosure and you must pass round the left-hand side of it. There you come to a signpost and a narrow path continuing upvalley over more pastureland. Ahead a jagged ridge (Meidzand) offers an intriguing skyline.

The path winds steadily up the hillside veering slightly left, and then follows beside a small stream for a short distance to another footpath junction. (The right-hand trail goes to a small tarn, Lac de Combavert 2442m.) Continue straight ahead; the way is marked with MP painted in blue lettering on a rock.

131

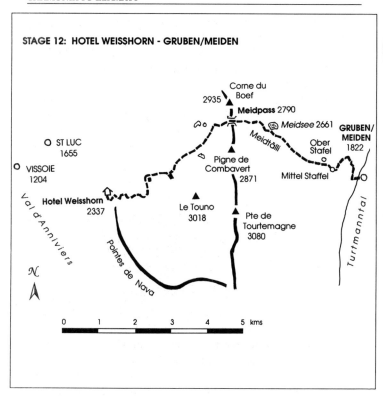

STAGE 12: HOTEL WEISSHORN - GRUBEN/MEIDEN

This brings you into a wild upper mountain basin with raw crags and screes above. The path adopts a comfortable gradient and zig-zags to the ridge, gaining **MEIDPASS** (2790m 2 hours 15 mins) with its starkly contrasting views. Just before reaching the pass you gaze back to the distant Mont Blanc de Cheilon, Grand Combin and even Mont Blanc itself. (It seems a long time since you left the base of that great dome.) But now to the south-east one looks over another somewhat desolate, stony wasteland, to more big snow and ice peaks. The Brunegghorn (3833m) and Weisshorn again look particularly impressive.

132

Meidpass is a narrow, stony saddle slung between upstanding blocks that appear quite rotten. Cornet du Boef, or Meidspitz, to the north, Pigne de Combavert to the south. The way down to the [1] Turtmanntal on the eastern side of the pass is an easy zig-zag route that soon strikes leftwards to the edge of the tarn of Meidsee (2661m). You then descend into a modest pastureland on a clear path with the Meidhorn (2875m) guarding it on the right.

There was no wind, no breeze, no sound of streams or falling stones, nor of marmots, sheep or cowbells. We were both so struck by the overpowering sense of peace and stillness that we stopped for a minute and listened; holding our breath against the day. And it was true; it was as though even the Earth itself had ceased to spin. As though all and everything had momentarily been frozen in time. There were no sounds. Before I had always believed that there was no such thing as silence beyond death itself. But this was the nearest I had ever come to total soundlessness. Straining every sense I became only aware of the blood surging through my veins. Beyond that, a deafening hush. We broke the stillness and continued down. Into the zone of silence.

The path leads easily to an alp hamlet at 2334m (**OBER STAFEL** - the 'upper alp'), beyond which you come to a lip of hillside and drop steeply to the lower alp (**MITTEL STAFEL**) with a grand view upvalley to the Turtmann glacier. From the hillside lip you can see way off to the left to the glaciers of Wildstrubel and Balmhorn in the Bernese Alps, and to the cone of the lovely [2] Bietschhorn (3934m) which rises above the Lötschental on the far side of the unseen Rhône valley.

Below Mittel Stafel you enter a forest of stone pine and larch and descend pleasantly and without too much knee-jarring, to reach the valley floor. Cross the Turtmann stream by a bridge and walk up the opposite slope to reach the small and attractive village of **GRUBEN-MEIDEN**. From the valley once again the [3] Weisshorn can be seen gleaming from the south.

[4] **GRUBEN** (1822m 4 hours) *Accommodation, refreshments, shop. Accommodation at Hotel Schwarzhorn (beds & matratzenlager/dortoirs)*

Gruben/Meiden in the Turtmanntal

(028) 42 14 14 - open June to October. Matratzenlager/dortoir also at Restaurant Waldesruh (5 minutes down valley from the village) (028 42 13 27.

* * *

Places or Features of Interest Along the Way:

1. **TURTMANNTAL:** This is one of the shortest valleys of the Pennine Alps and one of the least developed. It rises in the south where the combined ridges of Brunegghorn, Bishorn and Tête Milon form a lofty wall that never drops below 3500 metres. (The Weisshorn rises above and to the south of Bishorn and Tête Milon.) The Turtmann and Brunegg glaciers sweep down from this wall and weld together beneath Les Diablons. Below this junction, on the right bank of the glacier, stands the Turtmann hut (2520m 50 places $2^1/2$ hours from Gruben). The valley is a pastoral one with a few farms and small hamlets. Cattle graze the lower pastures, sheep roam higher on the hillsides. There is no Postbus service into the

valley.

2. BIETSCHHORN: This impressive peak, seen far to the north, stands high above the tranquil Lötschental which it dominates by its powerful presence. The peak is 3934 metres high and was first climbed by Leslie Stephen and his guides in 1859.

3. WEISSHORN: Yet again this graceful mountain announces its presence. In his classic book *The Playground of Europe*, Leslie Stephen (see above) wrote of the view of it from the valley just outside Gruben: "Above us rose the Weisshorn in one of the most sublime aspects of that almost faultless mountain. The Turtmann glacier, broad and white with deep regular crevasses, formed a noble approach, like the staircase of some superb palace. Above this rose the huge mass of the mountain, firm and solid as though its architect had wished to eclipse the Pyramids. And, higher still, its lofty crest, jagged and apparently swaying from side to side, seemed to be tossed into the blue atmosphere far above the reach of mortal man. Nowhere have I seen a more delicate combination of mountain massiveness, with soaring and delicately carved pinnacles pushed to the verge of extravagance."

4. GRUBEN: Also known as Meiden, this small village is the only one in the valley proper (Oberems and Unterems are at the entrance). It consists of a neat cluster of houses, trim white chapel and hotel above flood-level on the right bank of the Turtmann stream, idyllically placed between the Meidpass and Augstbordpass by which you leave the valley. The small store near Hotel Schwarzhorn stocks a variety of goods.

STAGE 13:
GRUBEN-MEIDEN - AUGSTBORDPASS - ST NIKLAUS

Distance:	16 kilometres
Time:	7½ hours
Start altitude:	1822m *High point:* Augstbordpass 2894m
Height gain:	1072m *Height loss:* 1767m
Map:	L.S. 5006 Matterhorn - Mischabel 1:50,000
Accommodation:	Jungen (Jungu; 5½ hours) - beds & dortoir (matratzenlager)
	St Niklaus - hotels, pensions
Transport option:	Cable-car (Jungen-St Niklaus)

This penultimate stage is, to my mind, the finest of them all and a walk to stand comparison with almost any other day's outing in the Pennine Alps. It has so many contrasts, so many features that capture one's attention. It has history, too, for the Augstbordpass which links the Turtmanntal with the Mattertal was used from the Middle Ages onward as an important trading route between the Rhône valley and Italy; a route that originally continued from St Niklaus to Zermatt and over the glacial Theodule Pass beside the Matterhorn.

The crossing of the final pass on the Chamonix to Zermatt route is a highlight in every sense of the word. It's most enjoyable throughout and never as demanding as the amount of height gain and loss might suggest. It leads through spacious woodland, over high pastures and into a stony wilderness, but then opens to some of the loveliest views in all Switzerland. The Matterhorn does not feature in these views, though, preferring instead to hide its graceful form until the very end. But other high peaks - notably the Dom (the highest peak entirely in Switzerland) and Weisshorn appear regal in their permanent wintry raiments, while the Mattertal itself is seen as an incredibly deep trench of greenery walled by grey rock and forest another world away.

On the approach to the Augstbordpass with
the Meidpass in the background

*Then comes the descent into that world, and this too is full of pleasures
and the odd surprise; none greater or more beautiful than the discovery of
the little hamlet of Jungen clinging to the desperately steep mountain
slopes high above St Niklaus. Not an unreal tourist haunt, this artist's
delight is a living, working, daily active alp hamlet, and one of the last such
remote farming communities to be met on the Walker's Haute Route.*

*From Jungen the path plunges again into forest, dropping among
birdsong and heavy fragrance into the shadowed depths of the Mattertal.*
Note: *There are no opportunities for refreshment between Gruben and
Jungen, 5½ hours apart.*

* * *

The way to the Augstbordpass begins on the south side of Hotel
Schwarzhorn and leads uphill as a grassy trail heading towards
sparse woods of larch and pine. It's a kind path, thoughtful and
generous with its long weaving zig-zags, and you gain height
without too much effort.

In a little under an hour you will arrive at a four-way path

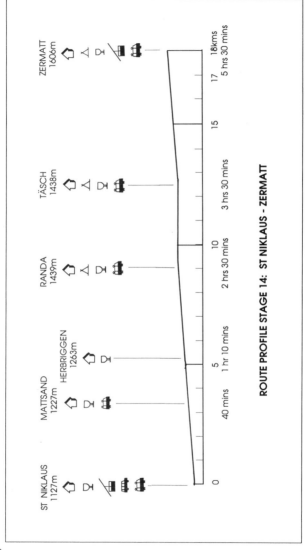

ST NIKLAUS 1127m

MATTSAND 1227m

HERBRIGGEN 1263m

RANDA 1439m

TÄSCH 1438m

ZERMATT 1606m

0 — 40 mins

5 — 1 hr 10 mins

2 hrs 30 mins

10

3 hrs 30 mins

15

17 — 5 hrs 30 mins

18kms

ROUTE PROFILE STAGE 14: ST NIKLAUS - ZERMATT

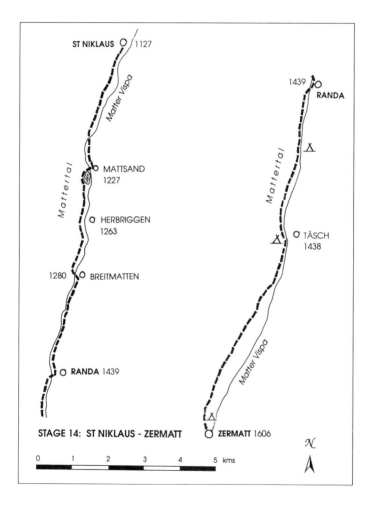

ST NIKLAUS ⭕ 1127

Matter Vispa

Mattertal

⭕ MATTSAND
1227

⭕ HERBRIGGEN
1263

1280 ⭕ BREITMATTEN

⭕ RANDA 1439

1439 ⭕ RANDA

Mattertal

⭕ TÄSCH
1438

Matter Vispa

⭕ ZERMATT 1606

STAGE 14: ST NIKLAUS - ZERMATT

0   1   2   3   4   5   kms

𝒩
▲

junction (**GRÜOBUALP** 2151m 50 mins). Ignore alternatives and continue straight ahead uphill. (The right-hand option goes to the Turtmann hut.) Emerging from the woods pass above a lone hut and wind up to an open shelf of hillside occupied by two alp buildings (**OBER GRÜOBU STAFEL** 2369m) with wide views across the valley to the Meidpass crossed on Stage 12.

The path continues, passing to the right of the huts and heading uphill to the left of a stream in the hanging valley of Grüobtälli. Still happily without any unduly steep sections, you rise to a lumpy inner region with screes lining the southern wall of peaks, and grassy hummocks elsewhere littered with grey-green lichened rocks. As with the basin below the Meidpass, this area too is a zone of silence where on a windless day few sounds intrude.

In about 2½ hours the trail steepens a little as you rise over a rocky step, then descend slightly to skirt a small pond before rising again, this time at a steady incline on the final stretch to the last pass of the long walk.

AUGSTBORDPASS (2894m 3 hours) overlooks a wild and rock-strewn wilderness, a landscape of austere beauty; but ahead in the distance rises the pointed, glacier-draped [1] Fletschhorn (3919m) above the vague hint of the Saastal, while in the middle distance northern outliers of the great [2] Mischabel wall, with Balfrin and Ulrichshorn above the Ried glacier, spread in a lavish show of grandeur, promising much.

Given sufficient time (plus energy and inclination), the Schwarzhorn to the north would be worth a visit. (1 hour from the pass; head off up it to the left.) The panorama it affords is on a grand scale, and those who know it claim it to be one of the great viewpoints of the Alps - "one of surpassing magnificence": to the north a memorable spread of the Bernese Alps, including Finsteraarhorn and Doldenhorn; to the south the view takes in Monte Rosa, Liskamm, Weisshorn and Dent Blanche; and to the east the Ticino Alps blaze a blue horizon, while nearer to hand the Mischabel chain, Weissmeis, Fletschhorn and Monte Leone draw shadows from the sun.

A clear path drops in zig-zags to a stony bowl on the eastern side; the cirque that cups the Inners Tälli. Steeply at first, the way eases lower down and 25 minutes from the pass squeezes through a rocky cleft, emerging to scanty grass littered with rocks. About 10 minutes later you come to a junction of paths, taking the right-hand option (signposted to Jungen and St Niklaus) that slopes down and then veers over to the right-hand side of the valley, crossing the Embdbach stream.

The route now embarks upon a fine, gently rising traverse of the southern flanks of the valley, heading east across a slope of boulders and rocks. But it's a well-made path and it brings you to a shoulder of mountain at 2488 metres where you gain a first sighting of the deep cut of the [3] Mattertal. Off to the left can be seen the [4] Grosser Aletschgletscher.

Continuing round the mountainside the path becomes rather narrow and a little exposed. It climbs one or two rocky steps and then turns the ridge (**TROÜRA** 2657m 4½ hours), and there before you is one of those sights that is so overwhelmingly powerful that all else is temporarily forgotten in a surge of admiration.

Across the gulf of the Mattertal soar Nadelhorn, Lenzspitze and [5] Dom with the Ried glacier pouring into the shoe-horn trough it has carved above Grachen's green terrace. It is indeed a stunning vision of loveliness, full of drama and grace of form, a perfect symbol of mountain architecture. (Ruskin would have loved it.) Then, right at the head of the Mattertal, Liskamm, Castor and Pollux and the long white block of the Breithorn, with the smaller pyramid of the Kleine Matterhorn next to it, make a fine show. (The Matterhorn itself remains shyly hidden behind the black outline of the Mettelhorn.)

A few more paces and, most stunning of all, the Weisshorn yet again announces its domineering presence, dazzling the sunshine above and behind the Brunegghorn that rises in one immense shaft nearly two and a half thousand metres out of the valley.

This spur of mountainside, three hours above the valley, is surely the crowning glory of the Walker's Haute Route, a route that has presented one visual gem after another from start to finish. At least, that's how it seemed to us, for we found ourselves trapped here, spellbound with wonder, perched on a sun-warmed slab of rock with heaven all around.

Now the path becomes a paved mule track, but soon narrows again as the descent proper begins, winding down in long, undemanding loops. When you arrive at a junction of paths with a seat and a signpost (**UNTERE LAGER** 2255m), head to the right on a path marked Jungen Rundweg.

This slopes down towards the Jungtal, goes through a stone wall and then cuts back to the left, and follows the wall for some distance before swinging to the right among trees, and then twisting down to the picturesque little hamlet of **JUNGEN** (1955m 5½ hours *accommodation, refreshments, cable-car to St Niklaus*). This is a delightful collection of old timber chalets and barns, with a white painted chapel perched high above the valley. (*Note:* The map names this hamlet Jungu.)

As soon as we saw the hamlet from the path way above it, we knew instinctively it would offer something special, and it did. Coming down to Jungen reinforced that initial instinct. First there was the visual impact - a quintessential alp hamlet of almost black timbers with a long, dramatic view right to the head of the valley. The valley lay 900 metres below; the Dom (4545m) soared up to full height opposite, a white crust above the rocky Grabenhorn, with the Ried glacier peeling through its funnel; Brunegghorn and Weisshorn above to the right dazzled in the afternoon like sunlight in a mirror. We wandered between the buildings and, just below the chapel, saw a restaurant, Junger-Stübli, and couldn't resist stopping there for a drink with that view. Our plan had originally been to continue down to St Niklaus, but when we realized there was a bed to be had here, our plan changed instantly. St Niklaus could wait until tomorrow. We booked in and that evening studied the mountains through binoculars, catching sight of a light twinkling from the Bordier hut below the Balfrin opposite, and another at the head of the valley where a glow-worm-sized train was moving slowly against a black mountain shape towards the Gornergrat. A world remote from ours. Jungen was full of magic and we spent a memorable night there, enjoying first-class hospitality in a setting that was nothing short of pure enchantment.

Limited amount of accommodation available - 3 double bedrooms and

The splendidly placed hamlet of Jungen above the Mattertal

a small dormitory (*matratzenlager*) with 4 bunks. Bed and breakfast rates, light snacks, well-equipped kitchen for self-catering in the evening (bring your own food). Evening meals if booked in advance. Magnificent views. Open June-October. Reservations to: Familie M Füx-Pollinger, Junger-Stübli, 3924 St Niklaus. Tel: (Jungen) (028) 56 21 01 (or St Niklaus: (028) 56 24 08).

The path through Jungen leads to the chapel, winds steeply below the restaurant and zig-zags into forest. About 35 minutes below Jungen you will come to a footpath junction where you continue straight ahead (the alternative trail cuts sharply back to the left). Cross a rocky cleft on a footbridge over a stream which pours through it in foaming cascades. The way winds on, still through forest as it twists round the lower hillside, then between small parcels of meadowland to reach the railway station at **ST NIKLAUS**.

(6) **ST NIKLAUS** (1127m 7½ hours) *Accommodation, refreshments, shops, banks, PTT, railway (to Zermatt and Visp), cable-car (to Jungen). Verkehrsbüro (tourist office), 3925 St Niklaus (028) 56 16 15 Lower priced*

hotel: Walliser Keller (028) 56 11 60

Note I: Accommodation (gasthof rooms) are available on the outskirts of St Niklaus, and will be passed on the route of Stage 14.

Note II: An optional extension of the haute route goes from St. Niklaus to Saas Fee via Grächen, and is described after Appendix B.

* * *

Places or Features of Interest Along the Way:

1. **FLETSCHHORN:** Rising high above the village of Saas Balen in the Saastal, the Fletschhorn (3993m) is a mountain of some complexity and one which, though little known outside climbing circles, commands a certain respect. Its twisted ridges ensure that every view is different. Glaciers sweep down on each side between extended rocky spurs. Immediately to the south is the Lagginhorn, with the Boshorn to the north. The Fletschhorn received its first ascent in 1854.

2. **MISCHABEL:** The name given to that huge wall of peaks that forms the western section of Saas Fee's noted amphitheatre and makes an effective divide between the Saastal and the Mattertal, the Mischabel wall contains Täschhorn, Dom and Lenzspitze, with a spur going north-west to include the Nadelhorn. It's a consistently high wall whose crest nowhere falls below 4000 metres. There's a bivouac hut on the Mischabeljoch at the southern end, while the Mischabel huts (there are two) are perched on a rib of rock between the Hohbalm and Fall glaciers. The western flanks are served by the Täsch, Dom and Bordier huts. Only the northern outliers of the Mischabel group are seen at first from the Augstbordpass.

3. **MATTERTAL:** The Vispertal strikes south from the Rhône valley for seven kilometres to Stalden, where it forks. To the south-east lies the Saastal, cut by the Saaser Vispa river, while south-westward runs the Mattertal, the valley of the Matter Vispa. At its head lies Zermatt and the Matterhorn, of course, towers above that. The Mattertal is a narrow, deep-cut valley, flanked by the highest peaks

in Switzerland. The eastern wall is that of the Mischabelhörner (see above), the western wall contains such magnificent peaks as Zinalrothorn, Weisshorn, Bishorn and Brunegghorn, while the valley is blocked in the south by the glacier-hung mountains that run westward from Monte Rosa - Liskamm, Castor, Pollux, Breithorn and Matterhorn.

4. GROSSER ALETSCHGLETSCHER: Seen to the north as a great ice river on the far side of the Rhône valley, the Grosser Aletschgletscher is the longest glacier in the Alps. It flows for some 25 kilometres, draining such Oberland peaks as Mittaghorn, Gletscherhorn, Jungfrau, Mönch and Fiescherhorn. Some fine walks, accessible from Riederalp, Bettmeralp or Kühboden, may be had on footpaths that run alongside the lower reaches of this glacier.

5. DOM: At 4545 metres the Dom is the highest individual mountain in Switzerland, since the Dufourspitze on Monte Rosa (4634m) is shared with Italy. The summit tops the Mischabel wall. From it the Festi glacier flows steeply westward, while the Hohberggletscher falls to the north-west and is fed by the neighbouring Lenzspitze and Nadelhorn. The normal ascent route from the Dom hut follows the right bank of the Festigletscher, crosses the Festijoch and then makes a broad sweep up the head of the Hohberggletscher towards the summit. The Dom was first climbed in 1858, and received an early first ski ascent (by Arnold Lunn and Joseph Knubel) in 1917.

6. ST NIKLAUS: This is the main village of the valley, formerly known as Gassen. St Niklaus has a 17th century church with an onion-domed spire similar to many seen in the Tyrol. It's a busy place with a considerable amount of through-traffic heading upvalley to Zermatt.

STAGE 14:
ST NIKLAUS - TÄSCH - ZERMATT

Distance:	18 kilometres
Time:	5¹/₂ hours
Start altitude:	1127m *High point:* Zermatt 1606m
Height gain:	479m
Map:	L.S. 5006 Matterhorn - Mischabel 1:50,000
Accommodation:	Mattsand (40 mins) - pension
	Herbriggen (1 hour 10 mins) - hotel
	Randa (2¹/₂ hours) - hotel, pension, camping
	Täsch (3¹/₂ hours) - hotels, camping
	Zermatt - hotels, youth hostel, camping
Transport option:	Train (St Niklaus-Zermatt)

This final stage of the long walk from Chamonix is something of an undemanding tease. The Matterhorn is what you hope to see, but it keeps its secrets hidden until the very end. The walk, it must be said, is by no means one of the most scenic of the Haute Route, but it is not as uninteresting as at first you might suspect, for there are hamlets and villages, ancient haybarns and pastures and forests - and the river, born of glaciers and great snowfields, for company along most of the way. There are several opportunities to stray from the route for refreshment, and various places too with accommodation available should you decide to alter the length of this stage - or perhaps delay finishing the walk until another day.

* * *

From St Niklaus railway station cross the square and head to the right, then go left down a narrow street (there's a yellow waymark) to the main road where you turn right, upvalley. Walk along the road almost to the outskirts of the village (about 400 metres), and where the road bears left to cross a bridge over the river, break away

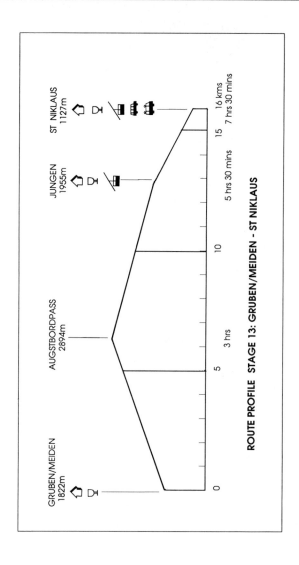

ROUTE PROFILE STAGE 13: GRUBEN/MEIDEN - ST NIKLAUS

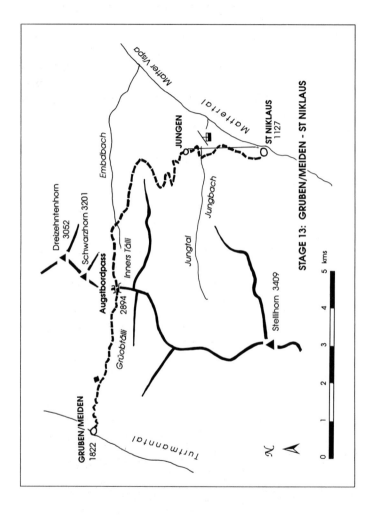

STAGE 13: GRUBEN/MEIDEN - ST NIKLAUS

to the right on a small side road between chalets. (Signposted to Schwiedernen and Topali.)

The way now follows what is apparently the 'old' road through the valley, bringing you alongside the Brig-Visp-Zermatt (BVZ) railway line and passing some typical old Valaisian houses, as well as some more modern buildings based on traditional architectural styles. (There is plenty of accommodation to be had along this stretch of road.) You pass under the railway and without too much effort come to **MATTSAND** (1227m 40 mins *accommodation, refreshments*) and, still on the old road, cross back over the railway line to skirt a large settlement reservoir. When the tarmac road bears left round the southern end of the reservoir, leave it and go directly ahead on a continuing track.

About one hour from St Niklaus the track brings you to a junction by a collection of haybarns. Continue upvalley along the right-hand side of the Matter Vispa river between more pastures, then down to a footbridge that leads over the river to **HERBRIGGEN** (1263m 1 hour 10 mins *accommodation, refreshments*). Do not cross over, but remain on the west side of the river (true left bank) on a footpath signposted to Randa, Täsch and Zermatt.

The footpath accompanies the Matter Vispa, then climbs a little beyond a barn and soon reaches a junction of trails where you bear left. Now you wind uphill among trees (some deciduous) on a very pleasant narrow path, before dropping again to the river bank (**ROSSWANG**) and across a footbridge to the main valley road on the edge of **BREITMATTEN** (1280m).

Unfortunately it is now necessary to walk up the road for about 30 minutes. (The former riverside path has been destroyed by avalanche.) Keep on the left side of the road to face oncoming traffic, and use the grass verge wherever possible.

In half an hour or so you will come to the outskirts of
(1) **RANDA** (1439m 2¹/₂ hours *accommodation, camping, refreshments,*

Note: In April 1991 a large rock fall from the mountainside above Randa demolished the railway and cut off the upper valley for several days.

shops, tourist information), a useful and attractive village which requires only a short diversion to visit. The main road, however, skirts the village on its western side.

Shortly before reaching the railway station, leave the main road and go down to the right on a feeder road, and cross the river just beyond a gravel works. Once over the bridge head left on a riverside path; attractive, mostly level and easy walking. This will take you all the way to Täsch in about an hour, and Zermatt in approximately three hours.

(2) **TÄSCH** (1438m 3¹/₂ hours *accommodation, camping, refreshments, shops, banks, PTT, tourist information, railway to Zermatt*) is seen on the opposite side of the river with its huge car park for visitors to Zermatt. Unless you require any of its facilities remain on the west bank and pass alongside the village campsite.

Until Täsch the footpath was gentle and undemanding, but now the trail begins to climb among woods, dodging to and fro near the railway. It's a clear and well-trodden path that leads directly to Zermatt.

Reluctant to finish the walk, we sat on a bench on the outskirts of Zermatt. Since first light we'd had rain and knee-high clouds, but far from being disappointed by this, we actually welcomed the non-visibility. It was a taste of justice, for until now we'd had almost perfect weather conditions every day. If views were to be denied us, this was definately the day for it. Of course, that meant no Matterhorn, but what we had experienced in the past two weeks more than made up for that loss.

At Täsch the rain had stopped, but low clouds still obscured every view. Seated on the damp bench outside Zermatt we reviewed the walk as a whole and concluded that it had been one of the most beautiful either of us had ever undertaken. (Between us we had more than 50 years of mountain experience.) Without doubt we'd be back to walk it again. And again. But for now we were in no hurry for it to be over. For all its undeniable attractions and for all its being the culmination of the walk ever since leaving Chamonix railway station late that sunny afternoon, Zermatt was not going to be another of those quiet, unimposing hamlets that had added riches to the route. We were about to face the crowds, and that would be a culture shock. So we sat among the clouds, not the crowds, and put off the final ten-minute stroll into town.

And we'd still be sitting there now if the rain had not started once more. (P.S. Next day we were back to clear skies and sunshine and so joined everyone else in heading upvalley with eyes transfixed by the sight of that great pyramid of rock. Our pilgrimage from Chamonix to Zermatt was complete.)

(3) **ZERMATT** (1606m 5¹/₂ hours) *Accommodation, camping, youth hostel, restaurants, shops, banks, PTT, railway (to Visp and Brig) etc. Verkehrsbüro (tourist office), 3920 Zermatt Tel: (028) 66 11 81*

Note: There are upwards of 100 hotels in and around Zermatt, several with dormitories. Before making advance reservations contact the Swiss National Tourist Office for an accommodation list. If you arrive in Zermatt without a reservation there is a free-phone hotel-booking facility at the railway station, and another at the tourist office across the square from the station.

* * *

Places or Features of Interest Along the Way:

1. **RANDA**: Situated midway between the Weisshorn and the Dom, this attractive village is being slowly developed into a low-key alternative to Zermatt. It stands above the main Mattertal road and railway and so is relieved of the pressure of through-traffic. From the village a steep path climbs up to the Dom hut (in 4 hours) and to the Weisshorn hut in 4¹/₂ hours. Apart from these lofty destinations, there are other good walks to be tackled from this valley base. The campsite, on the southern outskirts of Randa, has good facilities and fine views to the Zinalrothorn.

2. **TÄSCH**: Noted for its monstrous car parks which fill the meadows to the north of the railway station, Täsch is where the great majority of motoring visitors to Zermatt leave their vehicles before catching the train for the final leg of the journey upvalley. (Motor vehicles are

banned from Zermatt.) The village is so dominated by this traffic that it has little identity of its own. Almost everything here leans towards Zermatt.

3: **ZERMATT:** One of the great Alpine resorts, Zermatt's obvious success - in terms of popularity - is inextricably linked with the Matterhorn whose noble presence overshadows the town and everything to do with it. Edward Whymper's first ascent (on 14 July 1865) and the subsequent tragedy that occurred on the descent has been told so often that it is unnecessary to retell it here. It is a story that has been known to thousands of non-mountaineers throughout the hundred years and more since it happened, and is a consequence that must have played a commanding share in the town's popularity. But the Matterhorn is only one of many fine mountains visible, if not from Zermatt's crowded streets, certainly from the surrounding slopes. In fact there are more 4000 metre summits collected around the head of the valley than are to be found anywhere else in the Alps. It is, of course, a mountaineer's Mecca, even though mainstream activists long-ago turned their backs on the area and moved to larger mountains elsewhere. The appeal of the great snow and ice peaks remains as strong to middle-ability mountaineers today as it was in the days of Victorian pioneering, while walkers of all persuasions will find sufficient scope here to fill every hour of a fortnight's holiday based on the town. (*See Appendix A*)

AFTER-WORD

SO, ZERMATT has been reached at last.

Hopefully you will be treated to blue skies and sunshine, and be entranced by the sight of the Matterhorn beckoning from the south. A fine mountain of course, and one you will recognise instantly - even if you've never seen it before. It is, however, just one of many fine mountains you will have wandered past since leaving Chamonix, and although there are no more passes to cross and no more valleys to traverse, by now you should be physically-tuned and mountain fit, and your head reeling with a kaleidoscope of memories.

Those memories, no doubt, will mostly be stirred by the visual glories of the route - the broad panoramas of snowpeak and glacier, of green valley and sparkling tarn. But they'll also include recollections of overnight lodging places, of other wanderers with whom you've shared a path or a pass. There'll be sounds to remember too - cowbells and birdsong, the shrill whistle of marmots, the chatter of a mountain stream...and the sound of silence.

Experiences gained on the route will settle over the coming months before dreams begin to replace the joy of those memories. Maybe you'll wake one morning to a glitter of sunlight among trees, catch the smell of dew-damp grass - and have a sudden yearning to throw a rucksack on your back and be heading for a remote alpine pass again. Where to this time? To repeat the Chamonix-Zermatt route? Or to revisit the Pennine Alps of canton Valais in order to explore further some of those enticing valleys you crossed on this walk? (There are some real gems, to be sure.)

Or maybe you will hanker for a new challenge, for fresh horizons on another long walk. If so, consider perhaps the **Alpine Pass Route** which makes a lengthy traverse of Switzerland from the borders of Liechtenstein to Montreux on the Lake of Geneva. It's 325 kilometres long and crosses 16 passes, and along the way gives stunning close-up views of the Tödi and Titlis, Wetterhorn, Eiger, Mönch and Jungfrau; of the Breithorn, Gspaltenhorn and the Blümlisalp peaks above Kandersteg. A very fine walk indeed.

Or, for something rather different, try the **Jura High Route**. This long walk may also be completed in a two-week holiday. It begins in Dielsdorf, near Zürich, and travels 299 kilometres along the eastern ridge of the Jura hills to Borex, near Geneva. This is a quiet, unassuming yet magnificent walk. Not a dramatic high mountain trek, but a walk of surprising beauty - gazing across the low agricultural plains of Switzerland to the wall of the Bernese Oberland and, as you draw further south, to Mont Blanc and its neighbours.

And there is, of course, the well-known **Tour of Mont Blanc** of which you had a tempter at the beginning of the Walker's Haute Route - ten to twelve days round the Monarch of the Alps. Truly, those who love walking in the Alps are spoilt for choice. (Cicerone Press publish guidebooks to each of the above-mentioned routes.)

But for now Zermatt has much to offer. Maybe you have a day or two to spare before returning home and your appetite for mountain walking is as fresh as ever. If so, Appendix A contains some suggestions for making the most of that time.

APPENDIX A:
Walks from Zermatt

THE HANDFUL of walks outlined below offer just a brief sample of many to be had from Zermatt. Each one has its own special attributes and is highly recommended. Precise route descriptions are not given here. These are contained in the guidebook to the area: *The Valais* (published by Cicerone Press) which is readily available in the U.K. and is also usually for sale in Zermatt's bookshop.

1. **SCHÖNBIEL HUT:** This is one of the finest of all walks in the area which gives a full day's outing - there and back. The path leads upvalley to Zmutt and beyond in full view of the Matterhorn. It takes you across glacial streams and along the crest of a moraine wall to the hut which is situated on a grassy bluff at 2694 metres, and with superb views onto a world of ice dominated by Dent d'Hérens and the Matterhorn. (4 hours and 11 kilometres to the hut. Allow $6^{1}/2$ hours for the round trip.)

2. **HÖRNLI HUT:** The Hörnli Hut (3260m) is situated at the foot of the steep ridge on the Matterhorn from which it takes its name, and is where most climbers embarking on the standard route spend the night. A truly dramatic position overlooking a highway of ice leading to Monte Rosa. The walk is an extremely steep one, but rewarding for its views. The only disappointing feature is the cableway which rises overhead from Zermatt to the Schwarzsee Hotel (2583m). From Zermatt to the Hörnli Hut will take about $4^{1}/2$-5 hours. (2 hours if you take the cable-car to Schwarzsee.) Total height gain from the town is more than 1600 metres.

3. **FINDELN:** A short ($1^{1}/2$ hour) but steep walk takes you to the little alp hamlet of Findeln (2051m) for a classic view of the Matterhorn. Findeln sits on a steep slope of pasture to the south-east of Zermatt. The walk to it leads through woods most of the way, and when you emerge at the hamlet the Matterhorn view comes as a real surprise.

Refreshments are available here. It's a splendid place for a picnic, a great site to relax in and to reflect on the past two weeks of mountain experience.

4. **GRÜENSEE:** Reached by way of Findeln, this tarn is trapped in a shallow terrace of hillside below the gaunt moraines of the Findeln glacier. Views from the Grüensee look to the Weisshorn and Zinalrothorn. Refreshments are available nearby at the Findeln Glacier Hotel. Allow $2^{1}/_{2}$ hours from Zermatt.

5. **GORNERGRAT:** One of the great viewpoints of the Alps, Gornergrat looks directly onto Monte Rosa. It's an extremely busy place where you'll not find much peace. However, it is worth visiting and the train ride to it is highly recommended. (Choose a seat on the right-hand side of the carriage for the best views.) Broad and easy paths lead down to Zermatt in about $3^{1}/_{2}$ hours.

In the event of bad weather precluding outdoor activity, Zermatt's Alpine Museum is worth a visit. The town also has indoor swimming and enough restaurants and shops to keep you out of the rain.

*There are many good climbs around Zermatt like this of the
Rimpfischhorn. Lyskamm is in the background.
(Photo: Walt Unsworth)*

APPENDIX B:
Climbing from Zermatt

GIVEN TIME at the end of the Chamonix-Zermatt trek, and taking advantage of fitness, seasoned mountain walkers may be tempted to round off their trip by making the ascent of one of Zermatt's array of surrounding peaks. The Matterhorn is an obvious choice, of course, but there are plenty of others. Experienced alpinists will need no advice from me, but are directed to the Alpine Club guidebook to the area: *Pennine Alps Central* by Robin Collomb. The following notes, however, may be helpful for those with experience of climbing in Britain, but whose first visit to the Alps this is.

The first thing to understand is the scale of these mountains. After two weeks of wandering across their lower ridges you will have some idea of just how big they are, but it is only by setting out to climb them that the full stature of alpine mountains can be properly appreciated. They should never be underestimated. Unless you have a member of your party who has all-round experience of climbing in the Alps, and is competent to lead a climb or two from here, my advice is to leave well alone, or to hire a professional guide.

Zermatt has its own mountain guide's office *(Bergführerbüro)*, of course, with 50 or more official guides working from it. The office is found a short distance from the railway station along the main street (Tel: (028) 67 34 56). A variety of peaks can be offered, but it should be stressed that to employ a professional mountain guide here can be very expensive - although that may be justified by the knowlege that the experience of standing on top of your first alpine peak is likely to be one you'll always remember.

The cost of employing a guide for the climb itself is only part of the expense. Add to this the guide's food in a mountain hut (an overnight is usually necessary), hut fees for yourself and the guide, and hire of equipment - you'll no doubt need crampons, plus ice-axe if you've not carried one with you. These may be rented from one of the local sports shops. (The guide provides the rope.) It is also necessary to have mountain accident and rescue insurance.

1. **THE BREITHORN:** The easiest 4000 metre summit here (and possibly the easiest of its height in the Alps) is the Breithorn (4164m), reached from the Gandegg hut via the Theodule Pass in about 4 hours. It is an extremely popular mountain situated midway between the Matterhorn and Monte Rosa.

2. **THE MATTERHORN:** At 4477 metres, this great pyramid is, naturally, the focus of attention of all who visit Zermatt, and is possibly the one alpine peak all attracted to mountains would love to climb. The standard route by way of the Hörnli ridge is not difficult by alpine standards, but is nevertheless a serious route for novices, with several severely exposed pitches. (The route is graded PD. Numerous rock climbing pitches graded II.) One of the problems faced by climbers on this route is the danger of stone-fall; another, general to the mountain, is the bad weather it attracts. From the Hörnli hut, an average time to the summit for experienced climbers would be about 5 hours.

3. **MONTE ROSA:** Containing the second highest summit in the Alps (the Dufourspitze, 4634m) the Monte Rosa massif holds a number of very high peaks which are shared between Switzerland and Italy. It's an extremely snowy, glacier-adorned massif, with some lengthy routes on it. The Monte Rosa Hut (2795m) is situated to the north-west of the mountain, on the Unter Plattje rocks surrounded by glaciers. It is reached in 2 hours from Rotboden Station on the Gornergrat railway. From the hut the popular Dufourspitze may be climbed by way of the north-west flank and then along the west ridge in about 6 hours.

There are, of course, numerous other peaks in the area, many of which have routes of greater interest or challenge to experienced climbers. There are also glacier tours that would provide memorable days out. You need never go short of ideas in Zermatt.

EXTENSION TO SAAS FEE

CONTINUING THE Haute Route to Saas Fee in the next valley to the east of the Mattertal makes a natural extension, and one that was long recognised by ski-mountaineers on their classic glacier route. Unlike ski mountaineers, however, walkers wishing to avoid the icefields that form the great highway between Zermatt and Saas have to make a detour round the ridge system that creates such an effective divide between the two valleys. It's a detour of some consequence. A glorious scenic route along a classic belvedere *Höhenweg* that makes a worthy conclusion to a traverse of the Pennine Alps and a fitting finale to the walker's Haute Route.

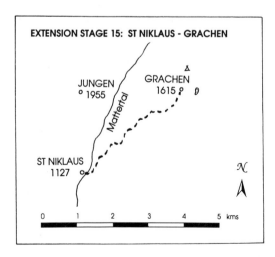

EXTENSION STAGE 15
ST NIKLAUS - GRÄCHEN

Distance:	4 kilometres
Time:	2 hours
Start altitude:	1127m *High point:* Grächen 1615m
Height gain:	488m
Map:	L.S. 5006 Matterhorn - Mischabel 1:50,000
Accommodation:	Rittinen (1hr 15 mins) - hotel
	Niedergrächen (1 hour 30 mins) - hotel
	Randa (2½ hours) - hotel, pension, camping
	Grächen - hotels, matratzenlager/dortoirs,
	camping
Transport option:	BVZ bus (St Niklaus-Grächen)

The first stage of the extension to Saas Fee is a short one, handy for haute route trekkers who have first visited Zermatt and find that they have two days in hand. It would be feasible to spend the morning in Zermatt (perhaps even visiting Findeln or some other nearby place of interest), then catch the train down to St Niklaus in the afternoon, leaving a two-hour walk late in the day. But Grächen is such a neat pretty village, with fine views and a delightfully sunny location, that a full day could easily be spent there. If the plan is to ignore Zermatt altogether and continue on to Saas Fee, then the better idea would be to spend the previous night in Jungen, rather than St Niklaus, thereby making a 3½-4 hour walk.

Grächen is perched on a sunny shelf of hillside on the eastern side of the valley, virtually facing Jungen across the depths of the Mattertal. It's an attractive, if strung-out village, with many pleasant Valaisian chalets hugging the alleyways and narrow streets. Above it to the south hangs the long tongue of the Riedgletscher from a clutch of peaks topped by the Nadelhorn - seen with the Dom above that, from the descent to Jungen on Stage 13.

From the main road in St Niklaus below the railway station a

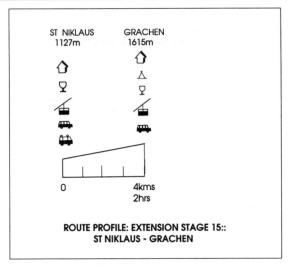

ROUTE PROFILE: EXTENSION STAGE 15::
ST NIKLAUS - GRACHEN

signpost directs the start of the walk down a narrow side street which leads between houses, crosses the river (the Mattervispa) and then bears left. Ignore footpath alternatives and continue to a major road. Cross directly ahead and walk along another narrow road rising among more houses. It curves to the right and comes to a staggered crossroads. Once again cross over and continue ahead, still rising among houses. When the road ends on the edge of woods a footpath takes you over a stream, then climbs among trees. On emerging from the woods this path makes a rising traverse of the steeply sloping hillside overlooking the northern outskirts of St Niklaus.

About 20 minutes above St Niklaus the path brings you to a collection of old timber chalets (**WICHUL** 1185m) where you bear right onto a narrow road. About 50 metres along this the road curves sharply to the right, but the continuing footpath slants off left and rises among pinewoods. It crosses the road again and maintains direction, still rising up the hillside at a steady gradient, goes above an old farm and, soon after passing a wooden crucifix, crosses the road once more. The broad path leads to **BODME** (1280m) where a narrow road is crossed and, immediately after passing a house on the left, bear left at a junction of paths by another crucifix.

Now the trail rises between steeply sloping meadows with views growing towards the head of the Mattertal and a fine collection of peaks. The path crosses a stream and soon after leads beside a white-walled chapel and comes to a road at **RITTINEN** (1455m 1 hour 15 mins *accommodation, refreshments*) opposite Hotel Montana.

Walk ahead along the road which exploits a natural shelf of hillside with a number of very pretty chalets and old granaries making the most of the views. Above to the right the Ried glacier is clearly seen; ahead is the wall of the Bernese Alps. Soon enter **NIEDER-GRÄCHEN** (1478m 1¹/₂ hours *accommodation, refreshments, shop*) and continue along the road until reaching another white-painted chapel. Leave the road here and take a footpath on the right beside the chapel. It climbs among houses and haybarns and forks by yet another crucifix. Both routes are signposted to Grächen. Take the left-hand option, in fact the main continuing path which goes up between meadows and farms and small granaries on staddle stones - all most attractive. This leads directly to the handsome, traditional Valaisian village/resort of GRÄCHEN. Bear left along an obvious traffic-free narrow approach route to reach the centre of the village.

GRÄCHEN (1615m 2 hours)

Accommodation, refreshments, shops, banks, PTT, cable-car (to Hannigalp). Verkehrsbüro (tourist office) 3925 Grächen (028) 56 27 27. Lower priced hotels: Alpha (028) 56 13 01 (b&b rates, plus self-catering facilities); Zum See (028) 56 24 24; Sonne (028) 56 11 07. Matratzenlager at Bergrestaurant Hannigalp - phone first (028) 56 23 81 - this is on the route of Stage 16, 1¹/₂ hours above Grächen, or may be reached by cable-car. Contact the tourist office for other matratzenlager addresses.

EXTENSION STAGE 16
GRÄCHEN - HANNIGALP - SAAS FEE

Distance:	19 kilometres		
Time:	7-7$^{1}/_{2}$ hours		
Start altitude:	1615m	*High point:*	Stock 2370m
Height gain:	984m	*Height loss:*	796m
Map:	L.S. 5006 Matterhorn - Mischabel 1:50,000		
Accommodation:	Hannigalp (1hr 30 mins) - matratzenlager		
	Saas Fee - hotels, matratzenlager, camping		
Transport option:	Cable-car (Grächen-Hannigalp)		

For a final day's walk the höhenweg (high path) linking Grächen and Saas Fee could hardly be bettered. It's demanding, visually spectacular and ever-interesting. In places the path is very exposed, with the valley a thousand metres below, but fixed ropes and cables are provided where necessary, and for those who have walked all the way from Chamonix there should be nothing too alarming. The whole walk is a delight, and the glacial cirque in which Saas Fee sits makes a fitting climax to this epic journey.

*   *   *

Just to the east of the village church a signpost directs the start of the walk to Hannigalp on a footpath heading between buildings (Chalet Wiedersehen to the right). The way passes several chalets, and goes alongside Hotel Alpina above which you pass beneath the cables of the Seetalhornbahn. A gravel track now leads into larch woods, rising steadily to a small tarn with Hotel Zum See on its shore, and very fine views back to the Weisshorn.

Continue uphill, and a few paces beyond the tarn you will reach crosstracks. Maintain direction straight ahead on a broad and obvious track that leads directly to **HANNIGALP** (2121m 1$^{1}/_{2}$ hours *accommodation, refreshments*). Hannigalp enjoys a splendid panorama of big mountains; not only those flanking the Mattertal stretching off to the south, but across the Rhône valley too, where the conical Bietschhorn dominates the long wall of the Bernese Alps.

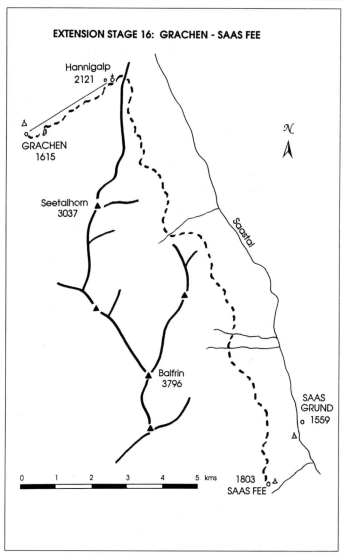

EXTENSION STAGE 16: GRACHEN - SAAS FEE

Hannigalp
2121

GRACHEN
1615

Seetalhorn
3037

Balfrin
3796

Saastal

SAAS
GRUND
1559

1803
SAAS FEE

N

0   1   2   3   4   5   kms

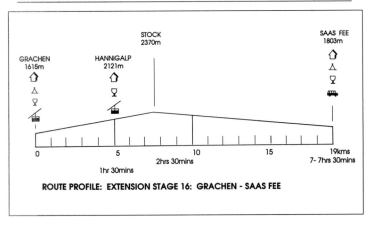

STOCK
2370m

SAAS FEE
1803m

GRACHEN
1615m

HANNIGALP
2121m

0   5   10   15   19kms
7- 7hrs 30mins

2hrs 30mins

1hr 30mins

ROUTE PROFILE: EXTENSION STAGE 16: GRACHEN - SAAS FEE

At another junction of trails continue directly ahead (signposted Högenweg Saas Fee[1]), soon reaching a modern chapel set on the edge of pinewoods with a picnic area beyond, and more breathtaking views. Here the path curves to the right and enters pinewoods again; a gorgeous path lined with alpenrose, bilberry and juniper - incredibly fragrant on a warm summer's morning. Skirting the northern spur of mountain which divides the Mattertal from the Saastal, continuing views are enjoyed between the trees; views which now include Böshorn, Fletschhorn, Lagginhorn and Weissmeiss above the Saastal, and the deep gorge of the Vispertal guarded by Stalden far below.

Curving now to the south the trail makes a steady rising traverse of the steep mountainside, the path narrow and exposed, but protected in the worst places. Cutting into rocky combes here and there, views are shuffled and reordered. In one place the path actually goes through a short tunnel blasted in the rock. There are occasional path junctions (one alternative route is the Höhenweg Seetalhorn), but the Saas Fee high route is obvious and generally waymarked.

In about 2½ hours from Grächen the high point of **STOCK** (2370m) is reached, and an hour later the path cuts back into a charming glen overlooked by the glacier-clad Balfrin (3796m). Here the path slopes down among trees and shrubs to reach a footbridge

166

over the Schweib-bach stream (2100m 3¹/₂ hours), then rises easily on the far side.

Rounding the corner of hillside to leave the glen, you look directly down onto a huddle of alp buildings far below. The trail now makes a splendid traverse of hillside, again rather exposed in places, then crosses a very stony section with waymarks to guide the route over rocks and boulders where the path is impossible to maintain. Beyond this, above Saas Balen, the path has been cut in the face of the mountain, with fixed cables again as a safeguard.

Then there is another delightful stretch with slabs and boulders interspersed with shrubs and a few dwarf trees. Saas Grund, and the outskirts of Saas Fee, come into view ahead; the first in the valley bed, the second on the edge of its partially-hidden glacial bowl. The path now slopes down across the grass hillside of **STAFELALP** (2084m 5¹/₂ hours). Ten minutes later cross a footbridge over a glacial torrent below the hanging Bidergletscher, and soon after enter the forest of Biderwald. (The signpost which gives 45 minutes to Saas Fee is somewhat over-optimistic.)

Through the forest you come to **SENGGBODEN** (2150m) and another trail junction. The Saas Fee trail continues ahead, winds through forest and reaches a junction where both options lead to Saas Fee. Take the continuing path (the alternative goes via Hannig and will be a longer route), which descends to a solitary chalet and then a crossing track. Go straight over on a narrow footpath. Thereafter all path junctions are straightforward, with Saas Fee listed on signposts. The way takes you down into the heart of the village, with the huge wall of the Mischabel looming above to the south-west, and a dazzle of glaciers and icefalls hanging in the south.

⁽²⁾ **SAAS FEE** (1803m 7-7¹/₂ hours) *Accommodation, camping, restaurants, shops, banks, PTT etc. Verkehrsbüro (tourist office), 3906 Saas Fee Tel: (028) 59 11 11 Matratzenlagers at: Touristenhaus Albana (028) 57 27 24, Alba (028) 57 27 24, Edelweiss (contact Hotel Gletschergarten) (028) 57 21 75 Lower priced hotels include Albana (028) 57 27 24, and Pension Mascotte (028) 57 27 24 (the two hotels are linked and share the same phone number).*

*   *   *

Places or Features of Interest Along the Way:

1. HÖHENWEG SAAS FEE: Also known as the Höhenweg Balfrin, this high trail has become a true classic. Originally a series of shepherds' paths, they were linked (by engineering methods in places) to create this recreational trail, and it was opened in 1954.

2. SAAS FEE: One of the premier resorts of the Pennine Alps, the first hotel was established there in 1850, but Saas Fee remained isolated from motor traffic until 1954 and its streets still remain free from tourist vehicles. There are large car parks at the entrance to the village. In the main square stands a statue of Curé Johann Imseng (1806-1869) whose name features in the annals of the mountain pioneers, for he was as well-known for his mountaineering exploits as he was for his priestly duties. Several 4000m summits look down on the village, but Saas Fee (indeed, the whole of the Saastal) is as rewarding for mountain walkers as it is for mountain climbers, and a vast number of first-rate expeditions are possible in the neighbourhood. (See *The Valais* - published by Cicerone Press - for ideas.)

*　　*　　*

HOMEWARD TRAVEL FROM SAAS FEE
THERE IS no rail services in the Saastal, but frequent Postbuses run throughout the valley. The homeward journey, then, is by Postbus from Saas Fee to Visp in the Rhône valley, where a fast train may be taken to Geneva. If you are flying home from Geneva airport, make sure you catch a train which goes direct to the airport, rather than face a connection from Geneva town station.

APPENDIX C:
Useful Addresses

1: Tourist Information Offices:

Swiss National Tourist Office
Swiss Centre
New Coventry Street
London W1V 8EE

250 Stockton Street
San Francisco
CA 94108

104 South Michigan Avenue
Chicago
Il 60603

P.O. Box 215
Commerce Court
Toronto
Ontario M5L 1E8

608 Fifth Avenue
New York NY 10020

Canton Valais Tourist Office:
Union Valaisanne du Tourisme
15 Rue de Lausanne
CH 1951 Sion
Switzerland

French Government Tourist Office
178 Picadilly
London W1V 0AL

2: Other Useful Addresses in Switzerland:

Schweizerische Camping und
Caravanning-Verband
(Swiss Camping & Caravan Association)
Habsburgstrasse 3
CH 6004 Lucerne

Verband Schweizer Campings
(Swiss Camping Association)
Im Sydefadeli 40
CH 8037 Zürich

Schweizer Hotelier-Verein
(Swiss Hotel Association)
Monbijoustrasse 130
CH 3001 Bern

Schweizerische Bund für
Jugendherbergen
(Swiss Youth Hostels Assn)
Postfach 3229
CH 3001 Bern 22

Schweizer Alpenclub
(Swiss Alpine Club)
Helvetiaplatz 4
CH 3005 Bern

3: Map Suppliers:

Edward Stanford Ltd
12-14 Long Acre
London WC2

The Map Shop
15 High Street
Upton-upon-Severn
Worcs WR8 0HJ

Rand McNally Map Store
10 East 53rd Street
New York
NY

Note: Swiss topographical maps are also available from National Tourist
Offices.

APPENDIX D:
Bibliography

1: General Tourist Guides:
Of the many general tourist guides on the market, perhaps the best and most
comprehensive is:-

Blue Guide to Switzerland by Ian Robertson (A&C Black, London. W W
Norton, New York. Published in 1987 (4th edition))

Also useful is *Off the Beaten Track - Switzerland* (Moorland Publishing Co -
Ashbourne. Published 1989)

Long out of print, but available on special request from public libraries, the
following general guide contains lengthy chapters on both the Mont Blanc
range and the Pennine Alps with some interesting background information:-
The Alps by R L G Irving (Batsford, London 1939)

2: Mountains & Mountaineering:
Numerous volumes devoted to mountaineering in regions of the Alps
through which the Chamonix-Zermatt route travels, are to be found in
bookshops and libraries. Those listed below represent a very small selection,
but there should be plenty of reading to provide an appetizer for a forthcoming
visit.

Scrambles Amongst the Alps by Edward Whymper (first edition 1871, latest
edition published by Webb & Bower, Exeter 1986 with superb colour photos
by John Cleare) - 'Scrambles' is *the* classic volume of mountaineering literature
covering Whymper's alpine campaigns between 1860 and 1865. It contains,
of course, the account of his fateful first ascent of the Matterhorn, but much
more besides of interest to walkers of the Haute Route.

Wandering Among the High Alps by Alfred Wills (Blackwell, Oxford. Latest
edition 1937) - Another record of Victorian adventures with guides on peaks
and passes of the Pennine Alps, as well as other areas.

The Alps in 1864 by A W Moore (latest edition published by Blackwell,
Oxford 1939) - A personal account of a summer's mountaineering with
Whymper and Horace Walker, in two volumes.

On High Hills by Geoffrey Winthrop Young (Methuen, London 1927) - Winthrop Young was one of the great pre-First World War climbers whose accounts are of high literary merit. This volume includes many references to the Pennine Alps.

Men and the Matterhorn by Gaston Rebuffet (Kaye & Ward, London 1973) - A well-illustrated volume dedicated to the most famous mountain in Europe.

The Mountains of Switzerland by Herbert Maeder (George Allen & Unwin, London 1968) - Large format book with splendid illustrations.

Alpine Ski Tour by Robin Fedden (Putnam, London 1956) - An account of the High Level Route ski traverse.

3: **Mountain Walking:**

The Valais by Kev Reynolds (Cicerone Press, Milnthorpe 1989) - A walking guide in the same series as the present book, it covers all the valleys of the Pennine Alps traversed on this route, except the Turtmanntal. 90 routes described.

Classic Walks in the Alps by Kev Reynolds (Oxford Illustrated Press, Sparkford 1991) - A large format 'glossy' book which describes, among others, the Chamonix-Zermatt route plus several day walks in the Pennine Alps.

Backpacking in Alps and Pyrenees by Showell Styles (Gollancz, London 1976) - Contains an account of a large section of the Walker's Haute Route across the Pennine Alps.

Walking in the Alps by J Hubert Walker (Oliver & Boyd, Edinburgh and London 1951) - Long out of print, this is perhaps the best and most readable volume of inspiration to mountain walkers. A large section is devoted to the Pennine Alps. Some information is naturally out of date by now, but the book is still highly recommended.

4: **Climbing Guides:**
Pennine Alps West by Robin Collomb (Alpine Club, London 1979) - includes many peaks that form a backcloth to the Chamonix-Zermatt walk as far east as Arolla.

Pennine Alps Central by Robin Collomb (Alpine Club, London 1975) - east of Arolla to Zermatt.

5: **Ski-Touring Guide:**
The Haute Route Chamonix-Zermatt by Peter Cliff (Cordee) describes the glacier route for ski-tourers

APPENDIX E:
Glossary

The following glossary lists a few words likely to be found on maps, in village streets or in foreign-language tourist information leaflets. It is no substitute for a pocket dictionary, but hopefully will be of some practical use.

German	French	English
Abhang	pente	slope
Alp	haut pâturage	alp
Alpenblume	florealpe	alpine flower
Alpenverein	club alpin	alpine club
Alphutte	cabane, refuge	mountain hut
Auskunft	renseignements	information
Aussichtspunkt	belle vue	viewpoint
Bach	ruisseau	stream, river
Bäckerei	boulangerie	bakery
Bahnhof	la gare	railway station
Berg	montagne	mountain
Bergführer	guide de montagne	mountain guide
Berggasthaus	hotel en haut	mountain inn
Bergpass	col	pass
Bergschrund	rimaye	crevasse between glacier & rock wall
Bergsteiger	alpiniste	mountaineer
Bergwanderer	grimpeur	mountain walker
Bergweg	chemin de montagne	mountain path
Blatt	feuille	map sheet
Brücke	pont	bridge
Dorf	village	village
Drahtseilbahn	télépherique	cable-car
Ebene	plaine or plan	plain
Feldweg		meadowland path
Fels	rocher	rock wall
Ferienwohnung	appartement de vacances	holiday apartment
Fussweg	sentier, chemin	footpath

Garni		b&b hotel
Gasthaus or gasthof	auberge	inn, guest house
Gaststube	salon	common room
Gefährlich	dangereaux	dangerous
Gemse	chamois	chamois
Geröllhalde	éboulis	scree
Gipfel	sommet, cime	summit, peak
Gletscher	glacier	glacier
Gletscherspalte	crevasse	crevasse
Gondelbahn	télécabin	gondola lift
Grat	arête	ridge
Grüetzi	bonjour	greetings
Kamm	crête	crest, ridge
Kapelle	chapelle	chapel
Karte	carte	map
Kirche	église	church
Klamm	gorge, ravin	gorge
Klumme	combe	combe, small valley
Landschaft	paysage	landscape
Lawine	avalanche	avalanche
Lebensmittel	épicerie	grocery
Leicht	facile	easy
Links	á gauche	left (direction)
Matratzenlager	dortoir	dormitory
Moräne	moraine	moraine
Murmeltier	marmot	marmot
Nebel	brouillard	fog, low cloud, mist
Nord	nord	north
Ober	dessus	upper
Ost	est	east
Pass	col	pass
Pension	pension	simple hotel
Pfad	sentier, chemin	path
Pickel	piolet	ice-axe
Quelle	source, fontaine	spring

Rechts	á droite	right (direction)
Reh	roe deer	
Rucksack	sac à dos	rucksack
Sattel	selle	saddle, pass
Schlafraum	dortoir	bedroom
Schloss	château	castle
Schlucht	ravin, gorge	gorge
Schnee	neige	snow
See	lac	lake, tarn
Seil	corde	rope
Seilbahn	télépherique	cable-car
Sesselbahn	télésèige	chair-lift
Stausee	réservoir	reservoir
Steigesen	crampons	crampons
Steinmann	cairn	cairn
Steinschlag	chute de pierres	stonefall
Stunde(n)	heure(s)	hour(s)
Sud	sud	south
Tal	vallée	valley
Tobel	ravin boisé	wooded ravine
Touristenlager	dortoir	dormitory, simple accommodation
Über	via, par-dessus	via, or over
Unfall	accident	accident
Unterkunft	logement	accommodation
Verkehrsverein	office du tourisme	tourist office
Wald	forêt, bois	forest
Wanderweg	sentier, chemin	footpath
Wasser	eau	water
Weide	pâturage	pasture
West	ouest	west
Wildbach	torrent	torrent
Zeltplatz	camping	campsite
Zimmer	chambres	bedrooms
- frei		- vacancies

ROUTE SUMMARY

Printed by CARNMOR PRINT & DESIGN
95-97 LONDON ROAD, PRESTON, LANCASHIRE, UK.